THEN AND THERE SERIES
GENERAL EDITOR
MARJORIE REEVES M.A.

The British in Egypt

WILLIAM K. RITCHIE

Illustrated from contemporary sources

LONGMAN

LONGMAN GROUP LIMITED

London

*Associated companies, branches and representatives
throughout the world*

© *Longman Group Ltd* 1973

First published 1973

ISBN 0 582 20432 1
*Printed in Singapore by
New Art Printing Co., (Pte.) Ltd.*

FOR ELIZABETH

Contents

TO THE READER   4

1 EGYPT BEFORE THE BRITISH   5

2 THE SUEZ CANAL   13

3 'YOU HAVE IT, MADAM'   25

4 DUAL CONTROL   31

5 THE BRITISH TAKE OVER   37

6 GORDON OF KHARTOUM   47

7 KITCHENER AND THE RE-CONQUEST OF THE SUDAN   67

8 EGYPT UNDER LORD CROMER   85

9 EGYPT SINCE LORD CROMER   100

   HOW DO WE KNOW   104

   THINGS TO DO   106

   GLOSSARY   108

To the Reader

Late one afternoon in November 1875 a man waited patiently outside a room in the Prime Minister's house in Whitehall, London. Suddenly the door opened and a head peeped out. It was the Prime Minister, Mr Benjamin Disraeli. All he said was 'Yes', but Montague Corry, the Prime Minister's secretary, knew what to do. Within ten minutes he was at the house of Baron Lionel de Rothschild, the great banker. Disraeli needed four million pounds right away. That afternoon the *Cabinet* had just approved his scheme for the British Government to buy shares in the Company that ran the Suez Canal. No one else could provide such a large sum of money so quickly. The deal had to be done swiftly and in secret. If they owned shares in the Suez Canal the Government would have a large say in running it. This was important to Britain because the Canal was the highway to Britain's great markets and possessions in the East. Casually the banker picked up a grape, peeled it and said, 'What is your security?' 'The British Government,' answered Corry. 'Then you shall have it,' was Rothschild's reply.

In this way Montague Corry loved to describe how he helped in the British Government's purchase of the Suez Canal shares from the *Khedive* of Egypt. Perhaps it did not happen quite like this, for you know how stories get changed when they are told many times over. At any rate from this time the British Government and the British people became involved in the affairs of Egypt. For many years they even ruled that country. This book will tell you how all this came about and what effect it had on the people of Britain and on the people of Egypt.

Words printed in *italics* in the text are explained in the glossary, p. 108.

1 Egypt before the British

Egypt, before the British took a serious interest in it, was a land where time seemed to have stood still for hundreds of years. Readers of the Bible and of 'The Arabian Nights' would have found there much that was familiar. In their clothes, their houses and the way they worked and thought about life in general, the people of Egypt were almost the same.

In the middle of the nineteenth century all this was quickly changing. An English lady who saw this change was Lucie Duff Gordon. Many British people had been to Egypt, but few had actually lived there for any length of time. Lucie Duff Gordon spent seven years in Egypt. She suffered from *consumption*, and so her doctor thought that the warm, dry climate of Egypt would help her. She was sorry to go, for it meant leaving her husband and two young children. But she knew that if she did not go she would soon die. However, to keep in touch with them she wrote many long letters, in which she told them about all the strange and fascinating people and things she was seeing. These letters were so interesting that many of them were published after she died in Egypt in 1869. They are very valuable because they tell us what an intelligent, observant woman thought about Egypt at this time.

Lucie left England in October 1862. She travelled by train through France and Italy to Leghorn, where she boarded the regular steamer for Alexandria, the chief port of Egypt. Right away she was struck by the differences between Africa and Europe. At the quayside, on by train to Cairo, and throughout that city's narrow, winding streets, there was noise everywhere. And how clear the light was! No wonder many artists came here

5

Lady Lucie Duff Gordon

to paint. But the streets were so dusty and the houses so stuffy. Most of all in Cairo she disliked 'the people's faces, the dirt, the horrible wretchedness, the whacking of little boys and girls who do all the work which Irish *hodmen* do for us'.

Cairo and Alexandria were full of all sorts of people, many of whom were not strictly speaking Egyptian at all. Egypt was part of the vast, sprawling Ottoman, or Turkish, Empire. Lucie therefore met Turks, Armenians, Syrians and Jews, who were all subjects of the *Sultan* in Constantinople. There were many Frenchmen, Italians, Greeks and Maltese, known to the local people simply as 'Franks'. There was also a small number of Copts, the descendants of the early Christian inhabitants of Egypt. All these people could be found in the country's few large towns. Most Egyptians, however, did not live in towns, but either in the desert – and Egypt is mostly desert – or in the many villages dotted along the banks of the River Nile. Visitors quickly learnt that these Arabs were the true people of Egypt.

Some of them, like the *Bedouin*, tended goats and sheep and wandered about the desert, but most of them were farmers. They were known as *fellahin*, an Arabic word, meaning 'diggers of the ground'. This was really a most unsuitable description for them, because they hardly needed to plough the soil at all. They lived mostly in the Delta, that part of Lower Egypt where the great River Nile flows out by way of many smaller rivers into the Mediterranean Sea. The soil here has always been so fertile and the climate so warm, that crops can grow without much trouble.

In ancient times the Greek historian Herodotus once described Egypt as 'the gift of the river'. Every year the Nile floods its banks. The water spreads out over the neighbouring countryside and deposits rich, dark mud, that is full of *humus*, which it has brought down on its journey of more than 4,000 miles from the mountains of Abyssinia after the winter rains. For thousands of years the farmers of Egypt have relied on this regular supply of fresh soil. All they had to do was to see that the floodwater was used properly. 'Waterer' would have been a better word to describe the farmer of Egypt, as he led the water by means of canals into those fields above the level reached by the floodwater. This was being done by methods that were centuries old.

In the Delta after the annual flooding of the Nile

Egyptian peasants irrigating their land with a shaduf

Boats on the Nile with their lateen sails

The *shaduf* was a kind of water crane. It consisted of a long pole, hung between two upright posts, with a lump of Nile mud at the lower end and a bucket attached to the upper end. The *sakia*, or water-wheel, was fitted with water-jars, which filled below and emptied above as the wheel went round, worked by a pair of oxen.

Fellahin had to keep the canals from getting clogged up with mud. This meant that they often had to work from morning till night, sometimes far from home, digging up the mud with their bare hands as they did not always have spades. Their families brought them food. They did not get any pay because all the land belonged to the *Pasha* and they had to work for him in return for being allowed to *till* the soil. The Pasha's overseers made sure that they carried out their work, and lashed them with a *courbash* if they slackened.

Thanks to this irrigation, farmers in the Delta were able to grow crops of all kinds. As far as the eye could see there were broad patches of wheat, maize and barley, and bright squares of clover, onion and beans. Rice was grown, and so were cotton and flax. There were also date palms and mulberry trees, for cultivating silk worms. With the boats passing by on the Nile, their huge *lateen* sails catching the breeze, the flat, monotonous Delta could be quite an attractive place. The fellahin were picturesque, too, dressed in their long, loose homespuns and felt skull caps, the women completely covered from head to toe.

The whole family worked from dawn to dusk. It was possible to see them all performing different tasks at the one time: the father, perhaps, sowing seed, the daughter busy with her *sickle* reaping corn, the mother grinding it with her hand-mill, while the son turned over the soil for the next crop with an old wooden plough. Yet life was not all work. There were fixed times according to Muslim custom for prayer and fasting, there were also the family festivals, such as weddings and funerals. And when work was done there was always time to sit round the village well and gossip.

Lucie Duff Gordon spent her time in Upper Egypt, where the soil was not so fertile but the people seemed just as contented. 9

She visited them in their villages. From the outside an Egyptian village looked like some kind of rough fort, perched on high ground away from the floodwater. The houses were practically all joined together, not built according to any plan, and made out of bricks of mud mixed with straw. There might be only one opening into the village and this would be closed at night by a wooden door. The streets were little narrow lanes, running here and there between the houses.

Though a farmer and his family might not have much to offer, a visitor was always welcome. Their house consisted of only one room, which was very small and very stuffy, for the tiny doorway was all that let in any light and air. Goats, dogs and chickens would wander in and out as they liked, while

An Egyptian village of mud huts

insects crawled in through the roof that was made out of canes or corn stalks cemented with mud. Here is how Lucie Duff Gordon described such a house:

> Can you imagine a house without beds, chairs, tables, cups, glasses, knives – in short, with nothing but an oven, a few *pipkins* and water-jars, and a couple of wooden spoons, and some mats to sleep on? And yet people are happy and quite civilized who live so. An Arab cook with his fingers and one cooking-pot, will serve you an excellent dinner quite miraculously.

Can you think what the meal might consist of? It was most likely eaten in the open air beside a fire made out of dried dung and corn *cobs*, the smoke from which kept away mosquitoes.

One house, larger than all the others, stood in the centre of the village. This belonged to the *sheikh*, or village head-man. His house was usually quite roomy, surrounded by well-stocked gardens, with vines and orchards of pomegranates, apricots and figs. If you were a guest in this house you might be given a room to yourself, and most likely a feast would be held in your honour.

After ceremoniously washing your hands and mouth according to Muslim custom, from a copper jug kept for the purpose, you would sit down on cushions, cross-legged, at a low square table. The meal would begin with a greasy soup, served from one large bowl in the middle of the table. Each person would sup in turn with a spoon from the same bowl. The rest of the meal was eaten with two or three fingers of the right hand – the left hand was never used for eating. Many dishes would then follow, such as fish and pigeons, and stews and salads of different sorts. On very special occasions a baked turkey, stuffed with nuts, or a sheep roasted whole, might be served. Throughout the meal it was considered good manners to pick up choice morsels of food and offer them to your neighbour. Servants, meanwhile, would come round with large jars and pour out water, flavoured with rose-petals. Wine was forbidden by their religion. The meal would end with boiled rice sweetened with honey. After the food was eaten, the company would then settle down to listen to music, played on a kind of flute, or perhaps watch some slave-girls dance.

Lucie Duff Gordon was always welcome among the local people and got to know many of them very well. Unlike most visitors she took the trouble to learn Arabic and to try to understand their customs. For instance, she found that though women were regarded as inferior to men they were not necessarily treated harshly. A man was allowed to have up to four wives under Muslim law, but he had to treat them all equally well. Indeed Arabs thought that Englishmen were very unkind to their wives and to women in general!

Lucie became a kind of local doctor. For miles around people came to her with their troubles. Some she could do little to help; for example, one woman asked to be made more beautiful! But she was able to cure others. Often they had been eating too many greens and working too hard in the sun. Sometimes their sickness was caused by ignorance and superstition; for example, they believed that it would bring bad luck if they washed their babies' faces. Many children, therefore, grew up blind for life.

There was much in Egypt to disturb a woman like Lucie Duff Gordon. She was saddened by the poverty of the fellahin which was getting worse. She wrote:

> I cannot describe to you the misery here now, indeed it is wearisome even to think of; every day some new tax. Now every beast, camel, cow, sheep, donkey, horse is made to pay. The fellahin can no longer eat bread, and I see all my acquaintances growing seedy and ragged and anxious. The taxation makes life almost impossible . . . Egypt is one vast *plantation* where the master works his slaves without even feeding them.

Such was the price of the changes that were taking place in Egypt at this time. Let us see what these changes were, who was responsible for them, and what part the British had in bringing them about.

2 The Suez Canal

A middle-aged Frenchman one day in 1853 was busy helping to build a country house when he received a letter with exciting news for him. There was a new Pasha in Egypt. After a busy career as a *diplomat* the Frenchman had retired in 1849 at the age of only forty-four, thinking that his active life was over. This letter meant that a new career was about to begin.

As a diplomat, Ferdinand de Lesseps had once served in Egypt, where he had made friends with young Prince Said, the

Said Pasha, ruler of Egypt from 1854 to 1863

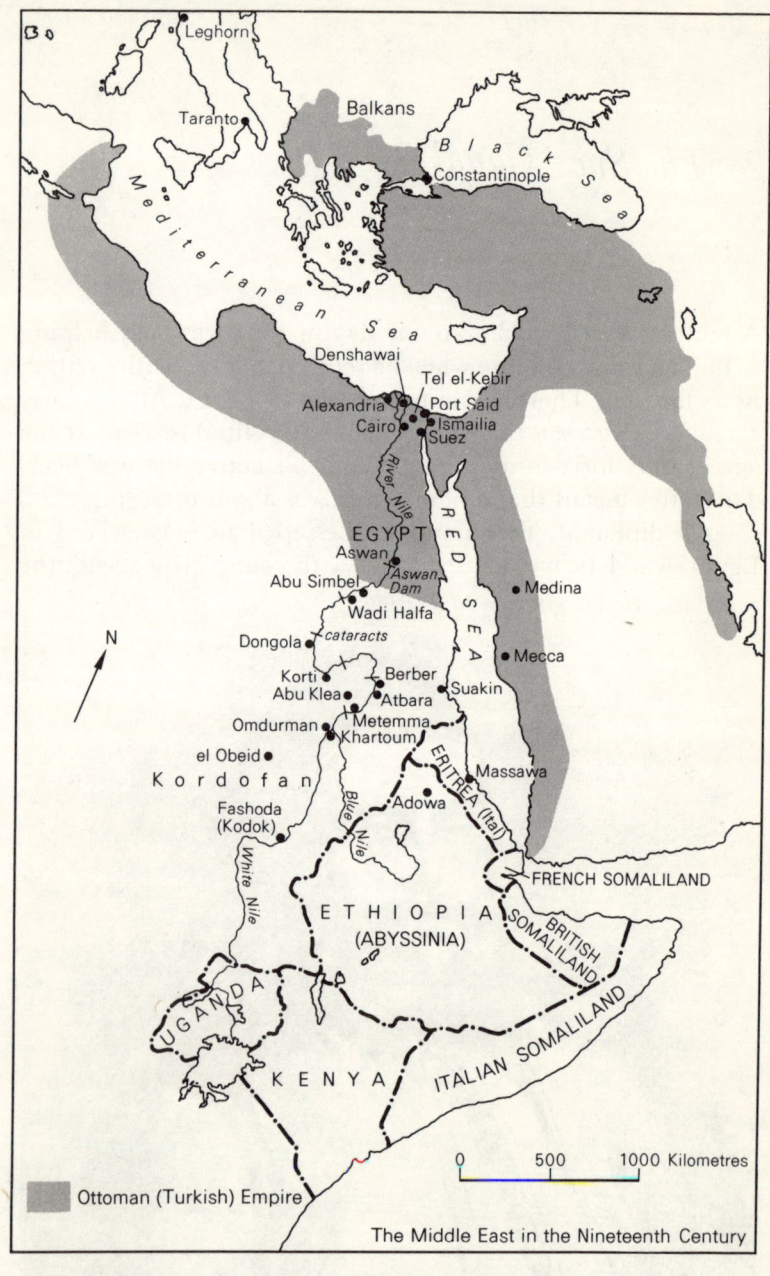

The Middle East in the Nineteenth Century

son of the Pasha at that time, Mohammed Ali. This friend had now become Pasha of Egypt in his turn. De Lesseps therefore wasted no time in writing a letter of congratulation. Said Pasha was delighted to hear from the Frenchman after so many years and invited him to visit him.

De Lesseps leapt at the opportunity for he was eager to tell the new ruler of Egypt of a wonderful plan that he had for his country. He knew that Said Pasha, like Mohammed Ali, wanted to modernise Egypt. Foreign experts had been brought in to improve farming, making cotton instead of wheat the country's chief export. They had introduced cloth-making and iron-smelting, set up a printing-press, and started schools and hospitals. Englishmen planned Egypt's first railway, and Spaniards and Frenchmen trained the army and navy. De Lesseps's plan for Egypt was to cut a canal across the *isthmus* of Suez, so that ships would be able to sail between the Mediterranean and Red Seas. Though he had no plans drawn up in detail, nor any idea how much the scheme would cost, he easily persuaded Said to grant him a *concession* and to supply him with men to build the canal.

Ferdinand de Lesseps

De Lesseps's difficulties only began when the British Government got to hear of his plans. They were very interested in them indeed. At this time they owned large parts of India, which brought them in a great deal of money from shipping, trade and building railways. Indian regiments helped to defend and to expand the British Empire. It was very important that India should be protected and that the route to India should always be safe. The British used two main routes to India, the Cape route around Africa and the overland route, which ran through Egypt. The Cape route, which was used by cargo ships, was easy to guard, with the Royal Navy and the storms of the South Atlantic. The overland route, however, was more open to attack. Passengers and mail were taken from Alexandria to Suez, where a steamer took them to India through the Red Sea and across the Indian Ocean. This had now become the quickest route. To protect it the British kept on good terms with Turkey, whose Sultan, remember, was the Pasha of Egypt's overlord. His permission was necessary before de Lesseps could start work on his canal.

The British Government did all it could to prevent de Lesseps getting this permission. The Prime Minister at this time was Lord Palmerston, a jaunty, sporty, outspoken old man in his seventies, who had spent most of his life defending Britain from enemies overseas. Like other statesmen of the time, he looked on the Turkish Empire as 'the Sick Man of Europe'. Slowly it crumbled away and seemed always on the point of collapse. What was to happen to this Empire was known as 'the Eastern Question'. The British were always afraid that the Russians and French would take advantage of Turkey's weakness to seize parts of its Empire – the Russians, Constantinople; the French, Egypt. The British had prevented this from happening already, but they were afraid Russia and France might try again. Both of them were, therefore, possible enemies of Great Britain. Palmerston did all he could to prop up the tottering Turkish Empire, because he thought it was the best defence of Britain's route to the East. Here now was a Frenchman trying to cut a canal that would literally separate Egypt from Turkey

Lord Palmerston, British prime minister

and speed the break-up of the Sultan's Empire. De Lesseps had to be stopped at all costs.

Palmerston was helped in Constantinople by the very able and experienced British ambassador, Lord Stratford de Redcliffe. He was so powerful that he was often referred to as 'the Great *Eltchi*', or simply as 'Sultan Stratford'. The Sultan himself was even frightened of him in case he summoned a British fleet to help him get his own way. Palmerston and Stratford used all sorts of arguments against de Lesseps and his Suez Canal project. They said that de Lesseps was a swindler: a canal across the Sinai Desert was impossible, it would get clogged with sand. Even if he was an honest man and a canal was possible after all, the cost would be immense. Besides, it would only be used to make Egypt a French colony, cut off from Turkey altogether. Of course, all the time the British were afraid that the canal might be a success, and that the French would control a waterway that could compete with the British-built railway between Alexandria and Suez. Anxious not to lose Britain's friendship,

'The Great Eltchi', Lord Stratford de Redcliffe

the Sultan eventually turned down de Lesseps's request – only in public, however. To keep on good terms with the Egyptians, de Lesseps was allowed to go ahead with his plans on the quiet.

First of all he had to be sure of support. He had already been assured of support in private from the Emperor of the French, Napoleon III, through the Empress Eugénie, a distant relative. Now, despite British disapproval, he went ahead to get more support. He went on tours of the chief cities of Europe. He wrote pamphlets and articles for newspapers, he gave countless lectures, pointing out all the advantages his canal would bring. In one year he spent £20,000 on advertising. Always he was quick to play on people's weaknesses. To merchants he said that his canal would expand trade and cut down costs of transport: the overland route was too expensive for heavy goods; the Cape route took too long, besides it was useless for steamships, because coal took up too much storage space, and there were not enough coaling-stations round the African coast to supply them with it. To shipowners he pointed out how there would be demand for more ships. The Pope was reminded that a canal would make it easier for missionaries to convert the

Emperor Napoleon III and Empress Eugenie

heathen tribes of Africa. The Sultan would surely see how much simpler it would be for Muslim pilgrims to visit their Holy Cities of Mecca and Medina.

In 1858 de Lesseps was so sure of getting support that he set up a company to build the canal, the 'Compagnie Universelle du Canal Maritime de Suez', with its headquarters in Paris. Though it was registered in France he wanted the Company to have shareholders from many countries. Most of the people who bought shares, however, were Frenchmen. Many of them did not have much money, but they wanted to support another Frenchman, especially one whom the British Government so clearly disliked.

Work on the Canal started in 1859 and took ten years to complete. A channel, cut from the Mediterranean through Lake Menzaleh across the desert to Lake Timsah, was joined to a similar channel that was led through the Bitter Lakes from the Red Sea. Since most of the ground was sand or marsh, very little rock-blasting was needed. To start with, however, a port had to be built at the northern end. Slowly one emerged out of the sea on a *sand-spit*, constructed with stone and lime that had

A bird's eye view of the Suez Canal. See if you can pick out the Mediterranean Sea, the Red Sea, Lake Menzaleh, Lake Timsah, the Bitter Lakes and the Sweet Water Canal

to be shipped from miles away. It was called Port Said, in honour of de Lesseps's *benefactor*. Fresh water had to be led across the desert from the Nile, in the specially constructed Sweet Water Canal. Where it joined the Suez Canal a town grew up, called Ismailia after Said's successor, Ismail. Huge camps had to be put up, with dormitories, canteens, *mosques* and hospitals, for the thousands of labourers who built the Canal. It was the greatest engineering feat ever attempted.

Though unable to stop de Lesseps Palmerston's government still kept up its opposition. Thanks to them none of the first shareholders were British. And when they got to hear that de Lesseps was using forced labour they raised a storm of criticism. This died down when de Lesseps quietly pointed out that the British had built their railway in Egypt in the same way. Work on the Canal in the meantime had been stopped. When it started again skilled, well-paid workmen from Europe were brought in with huge excavators. They were more efficient, so the work went ahead more quickly than ever before. Finally the British tried to persuade the Sultan to take over building the Canal himself, but this attempt to foil de Lesseps failed, too.

Thousands of Egyptian workmen excavated the Suez Canal like this

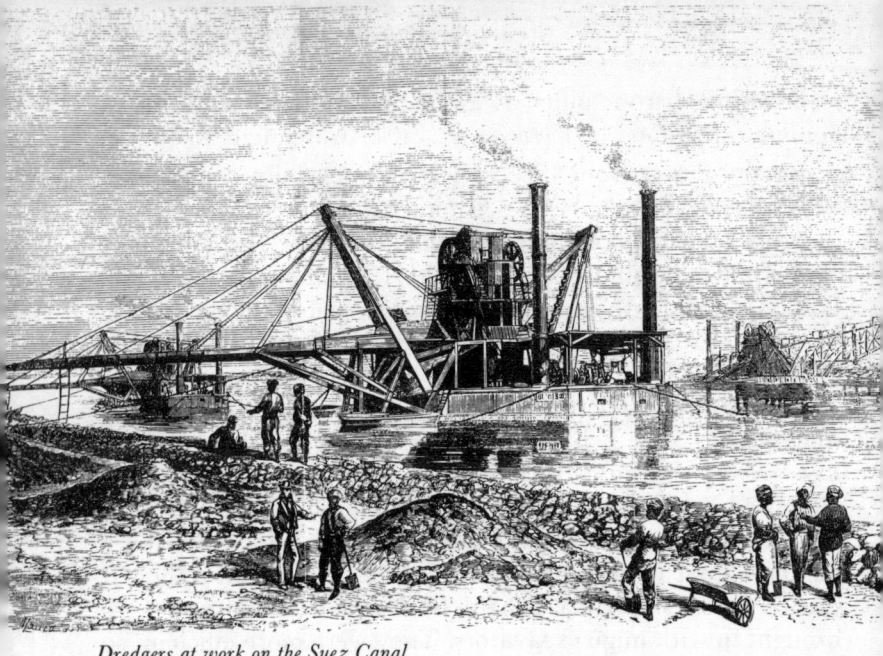

Dredgers at work on the Suez Canal

De Lesseps had many other problems to solve before the Canal was complete. Said, his friend, died in 1863, and it looked for a time as though Ismail, the new Pasha, might not be so keen to provide enough money for the work to go on. But Ismail soon became his most enthusiastic supporter. In the spring of 1869 the end was in sight. Soon the two seas would be joined. By this time Palmerston and Stratford de Redcliffe were dead, and the Sultan had formally given his approval. All the British wanted now was freedom for their ships to use the Canal.

The Khedive (as the ruler of Egypt was now called) planned a spectacular opening for the Canal in November 1869. No expense was spared. Distinguished people were invited from all over the world. Thomas Cook & Son, travel agents of London, arranged tours to Egypt at £30 a head. By the end of October the visitors were beginning to pour into Egypt in their thousands. It was a splendid occasion. The great Italian composer, Verdi, wrote an opera specially. It was called 'Aïda'; its subject was Egypt in the time of the *Pharaohs*, and it called for lavish costumes, massed choruses and colossal sets.

Early in November a great array of ships assembled off Port Said for the official opening, bringing representatives from all the leading countries. The guest of honour was the Empress Eugénie of France, because she and her husband had helped de Lesseps so much. Austria, Holland and Prussia sent members of their royal families too, but Britain was represented only by the ambassador to Turkey. On shore, thousands of onlookers in all manner of costumes had gathered to join in the celebrations. Huge *pavilions* were specially erected for Christian and Muslim services of thanksgiving.

On 17 November the opening ceremony began. Led by the French Imperial yacht, 'L'Aigle', with de Lesseps and the Empress on board, the magnificent procession of over forty ships made its way through the Canal with hardly a hitch. It was a superb spectacle. At night the ships were all lit up, while on shore there were fireworks and brilliant illuminations. A most extravagant dinner-party was held at Ismailia, where four thousand guests sat down to a dinner of twenty-four courses. Thousands camped out in the desert. And so until the end of the year the celebrations continued.

The procession of ships making its way through the Suez Canal just after it was opened

De Lesseps had finally triumphed. Without any skill in engineering or experience in high finance, he had built his canal. He had seen his dream come true with a mixture of enthusiasm, perseverance and charm. In later years he planned another canal, to link the Pacific with the Atlantic, but he died in 1894 before it was ever started.

The Suez Canal had cost around £18 million, of which Egypt paid more than half. You might wonder what the country got for this huge sum of money. Very little, in fact, except for the various services provided for the Suez Canal Company, such as railways, the *irrigated* lands beside the Sweet Water Canal and the new towns of Port Said, Ismailia and Suez. Indeed Egypt lost by the Canal, for the overland route, which had at least brought some passing trade, now fell into disuse. The country that gained most was the one which had tried hardest to prevent it ever being built. The first ship to pay *tolls* for passing through was British, and soon 75 per cent of all ships using the Canal were British. The Cape route was almost completely abandoned, because the new sailing distance from Southampton to India was shortened by over 5,000 miles. This meant a saving in time, depending on the size of ship, of between fifty-one and sixty-seven days. Prices were cut: whereas it would have cost you £140 to go to India by the overland route, you could now sail all the way by the Suez Canal for around £68. No wonder the British were now very interested in what became of this waterway to the East.

3 'You have it, Madam'

Despite high hopes, for the first few years after its opening the Canal did not pay. Much money had to be spent on improvements, such as making it deeper and safer to navigate. But when the Company tried to raise toll charges, Britain and other countries strongly objected. The plain fact was that not enough ships were using the Canal and so the value of shares fell. De Lesseps even suggested that some of the *maritime* countries might take it over and run it themselves, but this the Sultan would not allow.

By this time, however, the Sultan did not really count for much in Egypt. The Khedive Ismail was the ruler in all but name. Always dressed in rich clothes, he was known as Ismail 'the Magnificent'. No other ruler in modern times can have spent so much money in so short a time. His dream was to make Egypt great and a part of Europe. Within a short time, therefore, he provided his country with a new harbour and docks at Alexandria, a merchant navy, many lighthouses round the coast, over a hundred canals, more than four hundred new bridges, a regular postal service, and miles and miles of railways and telegraph lines. And these were only some of the results of his passion for modernising the country. Just as valuable were the million and a half acres that he reclaimed from desert and swamp for growing cotton and sugar. Exports from these rose in value from £4½ million to just under £14 million.

Ismail was particularly interested in building. 'Everyone has a *mania* for something,' he said, 'mine is for stone and *mortar*.' Cairo and Alexandria were transformed. Alexandria now looked like a port in France or Italy. An English visitor wrote about Cairo:

The city is lighted by gas, it has public gardens, in which a native military band performs every afternoon, and an excellent theatre; new houses in the Parisian style are springing up by streets, and are let out at high rents as they are finished.

In many other ways, too, Ismail tried to make Egypt up-to-date, such as building many schools, some of them even for girls, which was strange in a Muslim country at this time.

Ismail also extended the bounds of Egypt. He conquered the southern Sudan and parts of what are now Somalia and Ethiopia. He employed many Europeans as soldiers and governors. They were glad to help him because they wanted to put down the hated slave trade in Central Africa. Slaves bought in Khartoum could be sold in Egypt for £5 each. Suppressing slavery was not easy, because the Khedive himself employed slaves on his estates. One of the Europeans who helped Ismail to conquer new lands was Samuel Baker. After hacking his way through thick swamp and jungle in his search for the source of

Khedive Ismail 'the Magnificent', ruler of Egypt from 1863 to 1879, with his son Tewfik

the River Nile, he discovered Lake Albert. Another Englishman in the Khedive's service was General Charles Gordon, about whom you can read later in this book.

To pay for all his ambitious schemes Ismail needed more and more money. You will know from the first chapter in this book how he raised much of it, from the poor fellahin. They were set to work on the plantations of cotton. There was a great demand for Egyptian cotton in the mills of Europe because the American Civil War, which lasted from 1861 to 1865, interrupted supplies of American cotton. Cotton-growers like the Khedive became very rich.

Then the bubble of prosperity burst. With the end of the American Civil War European mill-owners were able to buy their cotton from the other side of the Atlantic again. There was less need of cotton from Egypt. Like other growers, Ismail ran into debt. He had to borrow from European bankers. The more he got, the more he spent, and they charged higher and higher rates of *interest*. In 1873 he was borrowing at the *exorbitant* rate of 18 percent. This means he was paying £18 for every £100 he had borrowed, so that he was paying out in interest £5 million a year. All he got in *revenue* was £8 million.

In 1875 Ismail had to find £4 million to pay his creditors before the beginning of December. He did not know where he was to get it. Then he remembered his Suez Canal shares. With more ships now using the Canal than in earlier years, the Company was making profits; the shares were rising in value and bringing in higher *dividends*. Ismail had 176,602 shares, about 48 per cent of the number issued. He could raise the money he needed by selling them. Secretly he began to discuss with *financiers* how this might be done.

As might be expected, word of a big *transaction* such as this was sure to leak out. Francis Greenwood, editor of the London newspaper, 'The Pall Mall Gazette', got to hear of it in the middle of November. He passed on the news to Lord Derby, the *Foreign Secretary*, but he did not show much interest. One who was very interested in these matters was the Prime Minister, Benjamin Disraeli. Some of his friends were bankers and finan-

Benjamin Disraeli, Lord Beaconsfield

ciers, so he knew of the Khedive's plans already. Disraeli was always anxious in case Britain's links with India were threatened in any way, and feared the Canal might fall into unfriendly hands.

A cable was quickly sent to the British *consul-general* in Egypt, General Stanton, telling him that the British Government was interested in buying the Khedive's shares—if the price was right. Ismail wanted £4 million. The Cabinet discussed the matter. Some members were against the purchase, but Disraeli won them round. Britain would buy the shares. But £4 million pounds—where was such a sum to come from? The deal was still secret and some French financiers were after the shares, too. There was no time to call Parliament to ask for its approval. To ask the Bank of England to lend the money would have caused a sensation; everybody would know about the deal. Speed and secrecy were essential.

This was where Disraeli's banker friend, Baron de Rothschild, of the great international banking family, was able to help. He agreed to advance the money in instalments. This is how Disraeli broke the news in a letter to Queen Victoria: 'It is just settled; you have it, Madam. The French Government has been out-generalled. They tried too much, offering loans at an *usurious* rate, and with conditions, which would have virtually given them the government of Egypt.'

We can understand why Disraeli was so pleased. He had just pulled off a great victory. Yet he was far from telling the truth. Disraeli loved to exaggerate. The French Government had not tried to buy the shares. In fact they had refused to help those French businessmen who were wanting to buy the shares, although this did not stop the Government of France from taking a lively interest in all that was happening in Egypt, as we shall see.

The news of Disraeli's purchase was greeted with approval at home and abroad. British newspaper writers were delighted that 'Dizzy' seemed to have beaten the French. Here is how the cartoonist, Sir John Tenniel, saw the British triumph in 'Punch'. A French writer, however, at the time pointed out

what few British people wanted to know: in buying the Khedive's shares, Britain had not gained control of the Suez Canal. The Government had certainly bought seven-sixteenths of the shares in the company that operated the Canal. But the company was French; in meetings of the company the Government, as shareholders, had only the maximum number of votes that any holder could possess, namely ten; and it was allowed only three out of the twenty-four seats on the Company's Board of Directors. Besides, the shares would not bring in any dividends for many years because the Khedive had *mortgaged* them already to raise money. It was not until 1895 that Britain earned any money from its shares in the Suez Canal, when they brought in £690,000. Their value increased. Fifty years later they were worth ten times their value in 1875, and earning annual dividends of around £1½ million.

No one at the time was to know all this. Besides, Disraeli had not bought the Khedive's shares to make money. He had bought them to stop the French from controlling the Canal. Some people said that this was a waste of money. He could have made sure that the Canal was safe for British merchant ships at any time by sending the Fleet to defend it. Others said that owning the Canal shares would lead to the British becoming needlessly involved in the affairs of Egypt. What happened next proved them right.

4   Dual Control

Having spent £4 million on the Suez Canal, the British Government naturally took a greater interest in Egypt than ever before.
When the Khedive asked them to look into his financial affairs,
Stephen Cave, the *Paymaster-General* was sent out with some
Treasury officials. They produced a Report, which, when published in 1876, had some very serious results. It showed quite
clearly that Ismail was deeply in debt. He had borrowed about
£100 million, a fantastic sum of money for those times. As a
result, European bankers refused to lend him any more money,
afraid that they would not get any back. They were right.
Ismail was unable to pay out any more sums of interest and
therefore went *bankrupt*.

The bankers and financiers felt cheated. They had been
promised interest on their loans, and to prove it they had
documents called bonds, issued by the Egyptian Government.
To make sure they would get their money, these bondholders,
as they are called, formed a body called the Caisse de la Dette
Publique, or in English, the Commission of the Public Debt.
They appointed two Controllers, a Frenchman and an Englishman. We shall hear more about the Englishman later. His name
was Evelyn Baring.

During the next few years these men gradually took over
control of the Egyptian Government. They attempted to put
the Khedive's accounts in order by introducing efficient book-
keeping methods and raising more money. They sold off to a
firm of French bankers rights the Khedive had to profits from
the Suez Canal. Taxes were raised. The Khedive had to cut his
expenses. He had to accept a *Civil List* and reduce the salaries of   31

civil servants and army officers. He had also to rule his country with ministers, two of whom were the British and French Controllers. They made him call a kind of parliament, made up of the leading men in Egypt.

Ismail became increasingly annoyed at these changes. His power was being *whittled away*. In 1879 he could stand it no longer and resisted. But the *bondholders* were too strong for him. They persuaded the Sultan to depose him and appoint Ismail's son, Tewfik, in his place. Ismail had therefore to leave Egypt and sail away in his yacht to a lifetime of exile, his remarkable reign over.

Tewfik was a man after the heart of the European bondholders. He did what they told him. Behind the bondholders were the French and British Governments, who held what was called a Dual Control of Egypt. In the words of an English official, Egypt 'was tied hand and foot, unable to move, almost unable to breathe, without the consent of Europe'.

People in Egypt grew to hate foreigners running their country. More than half the country's revenue went towards paying off the Khedive's debts. Poor farmers complained that it was they who had to pay most of the heavy taxes. Civil servants and army officers grumbled at having to put up with cuts in their pay. Rich and poor, ignorant and educated, high-born and low – everybody objected to their country being run for the benefit of foreigners. In 1836 there had been only about 5,000 foreigners in Egypt: by this time there were over 100,000. They had all the best jobs and were paid more than Egyptians. What was more, they were also *unbelievers*, who often ignored ancient Muslim customs.

The people of Egypt felt they were being *exploited*. Unable to turn to the Khedive for help, they looked for guidance to religious teachers and officers in the army. The man who became their leader was one such army officer, Colonel Ahmed Arabi. The son of a humble landowner, Arabi had served in the army since boyhood. By working very hard he had been quickly promoted to be an officer. He claimed, however, that he had never been given very responsible duties to perform

*Colonel Arabi,
the Nationalist leader*

because he was only a native Egyptian. All the important jobs in the army, as in the government, were carried out by Turks or Albanians, descendants of the followers of Mohammed Ali, who was himself an Albanian. Resentful at foreigners dominating his country, Arabi helped to found the Egyptian National Party in 1879. In their *manifesto* the Nationalists declared:

> Must Egypt be nothing but a geographical expression? Must her five million inhabitants be as cattle over which are imposed drovers at will? What they ask is to be treated as their brothers in Europe would wish to be treated if placed in the same position as Egyptians are placed. . . . Egypt wishes to *liberate* herself from her debts on condition that the *Powers* leave her free to apply urgent reforms. The country must be administered by Egyptian personalities of her own choice, without wholly excluding foreign help. She does not always want ministers representing this or the other European influence.

This shows how discontented people in Egypt were.

Arabi was anything but a violent man. In fact he was very quiet and good-natured, a big man, sincere and rather slow in 33 all he did. But he appealed to simple people. When they heard him make speeches they thought that he was putting into words all their feelings of discontent.

In 1880 Arabi became famous when he dared to tell the Khedive of the grievances army officers had against the Government and forced him to change his advisers.

Though some foreigners sympathised with Arabi and the Nationalists for what they wanted for Egypt, most were afraid of them. The bondholders thought that Arabi was planning to take over the government from the Khedive. They were sure that he would not be able to keep order and that they would not be paid the interest on their loans. French bondholders had no difficulty in getting support from their Government. At this time the French were just about to take over the North African country of Tunisia, though they did not want to interfere in Egyptian affairs on their own. Ten years before, France had been badly beaten by the Germans in the Franco-Prussian War. The French had recovered from the war, but they were afraid that if their army was ever sent out of the country the Germans might attack again. The French, therefore, looked to the British to help them in Egypt.

The British feelings about Egypt in those days of the Dual Control were stated by Lord Salisbury, Foreign Secretary of the time:

> When you have got a neighbour and a faithful ally who is bent on meddling in a country in which you are deeply interested – you have three courses open to you. You may *renounce* – or *monopolise* – or share. Renouncing would have been to place the French across our road to India. Monopolising would have been very near the risk of war. So we *resolved* to share.

Unlike the French, however, the British Government did not want to become directly responsible for collecting the debts of private people.

In 1880 there was a general election in Britain. The new Government, under Mr Gladstone, was even less willing to

W. E. Gladstone

become involved in Egypt. It would be too costly. Besides, Gladstone's Party, the Liberals, had been elected partly because many people were tired of Disraeli's costly interference in affairs overseas. Gladstone himself sympathised with Arabi and the Nationalists, because they were suffering under foreign domination. At the same time he did not want to lose the friendship of France. Should Britain intervene in Egypt?

People in Egypt were meanwhile losing all respect for the Khedive and his advisers. Law and order were breaking down. The Nationalists demanded some say in the government. This alarmed the French Government, who now pressed Gladstone to join them in trying to restrain Arabi and his friends. Gladstone tried to make this a problem that all the Powers might try to solve together. He failed. At the beginning of 1882, therefore, the British and French Governments together announced that they intended to help the Khedive to keep things in Egypt as they were.

35

The effect of this announcement was disastrous. People in Egypt were furious at this interference in their country's affairs. The Nationalists demanded control of the country's finances. Arabi was made Minister of War, in charge of the army. The Khedive was powerless to resist. Europeans were afraid of what might happen next. Business was badly affected, the value of property fell and many packed up and left Egypt. Everywhere speakers stirred up the people with fiery speeches and proclaimed a 'jehad', or holy war, against the foreign *infidels*.

Hearing of these events, the Governments of Britain and France decided that Arabi had shown his true colours: he was obviously trying to seize power after all, and he would not be able to restrain his hot-headed followers. They demanded that he should be dismissed, and sent their warships to Alexandria to keep watch.

Riots broke out there in June 1882. Howling mobs roamed the streets, looted and set fire to shops and houses, and attacked Europeans. The British consul was knocked down and about fifty Europeans, including a British naval officer, were killed. There was panic throughout the town. Mr Cornish, manager of the local waterworks, saw what was happening and later wrote home:

> I could see the harbour crowded with boats taking off hundreds of Europeans to scores of steamers, most of which appeared already crowded. I afterwards heard that many were thrown overboard in the struggle; it looked like they thought something unpleasant would happen to the *hindermost*.

A fund was opened for the riot victims by the Lord Mayor of London, as people spoke angrily there and in Paris against Arabi and the Nationalists. It was obvious that life and property for civilised people were no longer safe in Egypt. Could the bondholders still count on getting their money? Was the Suez Canal safe? What was to be done? Arabi could not be trusted to keep order, this was clear. Arabi would have to go.

5 The British Take Over

More ships were sent to join the British and French fleets off Alexandria. The British admiral was Sir Beauchamp Seymour, known as 'The Swell of the Ocean' on account of his great size. At the beginning of July he reported to the *Admiralty* in London that Egyptian troops could be seen repairing the forts overlooking Alexandria harbour, no doubt for use against his ships. Could he have permission to open fire on them before they were ready?

The Cabinet discussed for days what reply should be sent. Some ministers were all for bombarding the forts and for landing an army to protect the Canal. Others pointed out that in doing this the British Government would be responsible for killing hundreds of innocent people. Besides, Arabi might decide to take over the Canal in revenge. The discussion went on. Gladstone, an old man in his seventies, with other things, such as the problem of Ireland, on his mind, did not know what to do. He wanted to keep his Cabinet united so that he could deal with these matters. Finally, he gave way to those who wanted to do something quickly and firmly. Admiral Seymour was told to order work on the harbour forts to stop. Meanwhile, Gladstone was still in touch with the Governments of France and Turkey. The Turks, after all, were still officially responsible for the Government of Egypt. As usual the Sultan and his ministers, when faced with difficulties such as these, refused to make up their minds and did nothing. The French, who all the time had been making such a fuss about events in Egypt, now suddenly decided not to intervene any further. Their fleet was ordered to hold back. The British found themselves taking action against the Egyptians on their own.

37

Admiral Seymour went beyond his instructions. He ordered the Egyptians to surrender their forts. By the time they had agreed to knock them down it was too late. And so at seven o'clock on the morning of 11 July, British guns roared out over the harbour at Alexandria. That night the admiral reported back to London:

> I attacked the *batteries* and succeeded in silencing the forts at 5.30 p.m. I regret to say that the city of Alexandria has suffered greatly by fire and pillage. The Egyptians fought with determined bravery, replying to the hot fire poured into their forts from our heavy guns until they must have been quite *decimated*.

This is how Mr Cornish described the scene from the water-works on the edge of the town:

> At times the smoke entirely hid the ships and the town from us, but soon the wind increased and we had a good view. We could see the flash of the ships' guns, and the cloud of

Ships of the Royal Navy bombarding Alexandria

dust raised by the shell striking the fort or the ground, showed about the time the *report* reached us.

Houses near the harbour were hit. Fires soon broke out, some, it was said, deliberately lighted by the Egyptian army commander. The fires spread rapidly. For the second time within a month Alexandria was thrown into chaos. Frightened, screaming people rushed about helplessly to avoid the crashing shells and falling buildings. Some used the confusion to break into shops and warehouses, and looted as much as they could carry. Most people fled. At the railway station frantic crowds fought for places on trains, even clambering on to the buffers and the roofs of carriages. A stream of pathetic refugees poured into the desert on foot.

The next day Mr Cornish reported, after a day spent in the centre of town, 'There were but few buildings standing, the trees were nearly all scorched, blackened and shrivelled up. Every now and then a tottering pile of masonry came down with a crash.' By this time British marines had been landed to restore

A British sailor on duty in Alexandria

some order, Egyptian soldiers having been withdrawn. As a result of the bombardment about a thousand people were killed and five hundred wounded.

Back in London, Gladstone was still vainly trying to get other countries to be responsible with Britain for settling the Egyptian crisis. Reluctantly he decided to send an army to Egypt. The Suez Canal, it was argued, had to be made safe for British shipping, and Arabi had to be crushed. The House of Commons agreed and readily approved a sum of £2 million to pay for the expedition.

Plans to send an army to Egypt had been laid for months. *Intelligence officers* had spied out the ground between Cairo and the Canal, and a Cambridge professor, named Palmer, had been sent on a secret mission to make friends for the Government among the Bedouin tribes of the desert. He met a tragic end. He was robbed of his bag of golden *sovereigns* and murdered.

During the summer of 1882 the British Army prepared to land in Egypt. Many regiments applied to take part. The Prince of Wales volunteered for service, but his mother Queen Victoria, said no. Weapons, men and supplies were quickly assembled. Mules were ordered from as far afield as Italy,

India and America, and no fewer than sixty-nine troopships were needed to bring the 35,000 men from scattered British stations. British troops were brought from Cyprus, Malta and Gibraltar, as well as from camps at home. Native troops from India also took part.

The officer in charge of the whole operation was Lieutenant-General Sir Garnet Wolseley. He was a most capable general. Disraeli praised him as 'our only soldier'. He had earned his reputation for efficiency during fighting in Canada and in other parts of Africa. He was specially known for his up-to-date ideas on how the Army ought to be run. Ten years earlier he had helped to carry many of them out. Many senior officers loathed him for this. The public liked him, however, Gilbert and Sullivan, in their very popular opera, 'The Pirates of Penzance', made gentle fun of him as 'the very model of a modern major-general'.

As the troops began to assemble off Egypt towards the end of August, Wolseley began to put into operation his simple plan. The men were to be landed at points along the Suez Canal and

'The very model of a modern major-general', Sir Garnet Wolseley

having seized control of it, to make for Cairo, following the railway across the desert beside the Sweet Water Canal. In this way they would secure the main object of the whole campaign and also avoid fighting in the marshy *Nile Delta* during the time of the annual flood. To fool the Egyptians Wolseley let newspaper reporters who had accompanied the Expedition believe that he was going to land his men near Alexandria, at Aboukir Bay. Instead, they *disembarked* at Port Said. In a few days and after hardly any fighting the Canal was in British hands.

From his base at Ismailia, Sir Garnet now prepared for the advance on Cairo. Arabi had drawn up his forces, about 20,000 strong, around a long low hill, 120 feet high, that ran for about four miles north from the Sweet Water Canal. It was called Tel el-Kebir. The Egyptians had a most commanding position overlooking the surrounding countryside, and had dug themselves into trenches with deep dug-outs for their cannon.

The British Army made slow progress in the desert after such a brilliant start to their expedition. People at home became irritated as they scanned their papers for news of action. There was none to report. Sir Garnet refused to advance until he had made sure his lines of supply were in order. It was high summer, and the soldiers sweltered in their red *serge* tunics, blue woollen trousers and flannel shirts. They had been issued with light-coloured *pith* helmets, but some died of sunstroke because they would not wear their tinted veils and dark glasses.

At last the Army was ready. Wolseley could now carry out his plan to take Tel el-Kebir by night. It was a most daring adventure operation. To help him he had brought along a naval officer specially to guide the men by means of the stars. We can get some idea of what it was like from a letter that one of the men wrote home. He was a soldier in the *Black Watch*. First of all he described setting up camp after a tiring march of twenty-five miles in three days across soft desert sand under constant sunshine. He went on:

> We struck camp when it got dark and lit fires, and left our sick men to keep them burning to deceive the enemy, as we

were now told we were to surprise him in his entrenchments. After waiting on parade about an hour, the whole Highland *Brigade* moved across the plain. The order was spare none of the enemy, bayonet everyone of them as they would shoot us treacherously if we passed over them. We were told not a shot was to be fired, to rush over the ditches and earthworks and bayonet them before the alarm could be properly given.

The men marched in columns without making a sound except for someone who suddenly shouted hysterically. He was quickly

An officer of the Highland Brigade fighting at close quarters in the Battle of Tel el-Kebir

silenced and they marched on. Perhaps this outburst had alerted the Egyptians. The writer of the letter goes on:

Arabi was not to be caught asleep. His cavalry outposts had seen our advance four hours before, and every man was at his post. The day was just dawning when we mounted on a bit of rising ground and we saw, 100 yards to our front, his *redoubtable* fortress. We saw we were seen but we still thought to take them before they manned their guns. We fixed our bayonets and the sergeants their swords, and in about six seconds after the first two shots were fired, Arabi's artillery on the right and left front, and every direction, opened at once, and the blaze of rifles was horrible. We were ordered to lie down, which we did. After the short run of fifty yards we were all out of breath with the excitement and weight of our ammunition, which was very great. We lay about five or ten seconds as the foe could not see us and his fire was high.

Then the men charged, by no word of command, for none could be heard. The cheer that was given was terrific. The 42nd charged over the other fifty yards like tigers, sprang into the trenches while the bullets were whirring, whizzing and pinging like as many bees when they are casting. There is no use trying to describe it because it is indescribable. The pipes struck up 'The March of the Cameron Men'. The first man who fell was a man of my section who was hit in the chest. He threw his rifle into the air and fell back without a groan, quite dead. Over a dozen of our men fell in the attempt, but at least we got a footing on the top. Sergeant-major McNeil, Lieutenant Duff and Lord Kennedy, myself and two men mounted and stood calling on our men, 'Come on the gallant Black Watch!' And we leapt down into the fort and I fired the first shot, for we took the trenches at the point of the bayonet.

Our artillerymen and cavalry which followed us had filled in part of the trench and now came galloping up into the fort. We gave them a deafening cheer which they returned, galloped in front of us, wheeled about the guns, and poured *grapeshot* and shell after the now retreating army, we ourselves picking them off like rabbits.

The Battle of Tel el-Kebir was over. Many Egyptians tried to flee by train along the railway but were fired on by the British heavy guns. Cairo was taken the next day by some Indian lancers who made a quick dash across the desert. Sir Garnet arrived by train. By this time Arabi had fled, without having time, it was said, to pull on his boots. The rest of the Egyptian army were easily rounded up. From his headquarters in a palace in Cairo Sir Garnet was pleased to send a message home to the War Office: 'The war in Egypt is over; send no more men from England.'

Arabi's power was broken. When he was captured he was brought to trial. A *barrister* was sent out from England by friends to defend him. The charge against him was armed rebellion against the Khedive. Everyone knew that he would be found guilty. He was persuaded to plead guilty to the charges and so his life was spared. You can imagine that the British did not want to make a martyr of him by having him put to death. Instead he was sent into exile in Ceylon. Eventually he was allowed back to Egypt, but not for another twenty years.

Arabi died in 1911. A lady of the Khedive's court said this about him:

> He was never a good enough soldier and had too good a heart. These were his faults. Arabi was the first Egyptian minister who made Europeans obey him. In his time, at least, the Muslims held up their heads.

Today people in Egypt honour him as their first leader in the struggle for their country's independence.

The British were very pleased with the success of their campaign in Egypt. They had lost only fifty-seven men killed, 382 wounded and thirty missing. Egyptian casualties were much heavier: about 2,000 dead and many more wounded. The victory at Tel el-Kebir was a great boost to the British Army's morale: its reputation had fallen very low as a result of recent defeats in South Africa by the *Boers*. But once again it had won a spectacular victory, even although many of the Egyptians had been only raw peasants.

The British action in Egypt had many far-reaching results. Gladstone lost many friends and supporters. He had been regarded as a man of peace and the champion of the weak against the strong. A few years before he had made many stirring speeches in defence of the struggling peoples of the *Balkans* under Turkish domination. How could this man have sent a British army and navy to fight against the people of Egypt, who also wanted to be free? One of his most active supporters, John Bright, actually resigned from the Cabinet. After the shelling of Alexandria he described Gladstone's behaviour as 'simply damnable—worse than anything *perpetrated* by "Dizzy"!'

It is not easy to explain what made Gladstone decide to attack Egypt. Probably he did not understand enough of what was happening there. He certainly misjudged Arabi, thinking of him as a hot-headed military *dictator* who was unable to rule wisely. It is likely that he finally decided to interfere to keep his Cabinet together. He may have thought that if he did nothing those members who wanted strong action would resign. This would have meant the break-up of his Government, perhaps also of the Liberal Party; he would then have been unable to deal with a problem which he thought that he alone could solve, namely the Irish Question. Other matters were less important to him than Ireland.

But now Egypt had become a matter of the greatest importance. Britain's position in the world was changed. The Dual Control, which had been operated with France, was at an end. Britain's friendship with France had nearly been broken and it took over twenty years for the two countries to build up that friendship again. Gladstone meant to bring home the British Army as soon as the fighting stopped, but in fact the Army stayed in Egypt for three-quarters of a century. Much against his will he found himself entangled with Egyptian affairs. Whether they liked it or not the British were becoming the masters in Egypt.

6 Gordon of Khartoum

Shortly before eight o'clock one night in January 1884, three of the leading men in Britain were standing together on the platform of Charing Cross Station in London. They were the Duke of Cambridge, Commander-in-Chief of the British Army, the Foreign Secretary, Lord Granville, and that famous hero of the campaign in Egypt, Sir Garnet–now Lord Wolseley. They had all come to see off on the boat-train to Dover, a short, stockily built man of about fifty, who had the clearest of blue eyes. His name was General Charles Gordon. Together with his companion, Colonel J. D. H. Stewart, he was about to leave on what everybody knew was sure to be a most dangerous job.

General Charles Gordon at Charing Cross Station

General Gordon was starting out for the Sudan, a vast country that stretches to the south of Egypt for over 1,200 miles, and is more than four times the size of a country like France. At this time it was officially part of the possessions of the Khedive. Since the defeat of the Nationalists under Arabi, however, the Khedive had hardly any power in Egypt, far less in the Sudan. He was firmly under the control of British advisers, led by the British Consul-General, Sir Evelyn Baring. It was he who had asked that General Gordon should be sent out.

A rebellion had broken out in the Sudan and no one could put it down. It was led by a holy man, named Mohammed Ahmed, aged about forty, and said to be the son of a boat-builder from Dongola in the north of the country. He claimed to be the Mahdi, or Messiah, sent by God and the prophet Mohammed, to lead all men to give up evil ways and lead purer lives. Men like him had appeared often before among Muslim peoples, but none had ever been so successful in winning

Mohamed Ahmed,
the Mahdi

followers so quickly. A European who knew the Mahdi described him like this: 'His appearance was strongly fascinating; he was a man of strong constitution, very dark complexion, and his face always wore a pleasant smile.' Everybody noticed the strange space in his upper teeth, shaped like an inverted 'V', which was said to be the sure sign that he was a holy man.

The Mahdi's followers were known as Ansar, though Europeans generally referred to them as Dérvishes. They were utterly devoted to him. He insisted that they promise to stop swearing and drinking alcohol, and he made them give up all kinds of luxuries. They gave him all their money so that he could fight a 'jehad', or holy war, against those who resisted him. As a sign of their poverty, they wore a kind of uniform, a loose-fitting robe with black patches, known as their 'jebbeh'. He demanded absolute obedience. If they broke their vows they were severely whipped. They almost worshipped him, and even drank the water in which he had bathed, in the belief that it would cure them of illness.

People followed the Mahdi for different reasons. Most probably wanted a purer form of religion. Many joined him because they were tired of being ruled by Egyptian foreigners, especially as these employed Christian unbelievers to collect taxes for them. Others were former slave-traders who hated the Khedive Ismail for putting them out of business.

In the spring of 1883 it was reported that the Mahdi had captured the important stronghold of el-Obeid. With its large stores of food, rifles and ammunition he now had control of the whole of the vast, rich province of Kordofan. The Egyptian Government was powerless to stop him. As a result of Arabi's rebellion it had very little money and not enough trained soldiers. An English officer named Colonel Hicks managed to raise a small force of about 8,000 men, which set off from Khartoum to fight the Mahdi. Then the tragic news leaked out. Somewhere in the semi-desert south of el-Obeid Hicks's men were surrounded and wiped out by 50,000 triumphant Dervishes. Nothing seemed to stand in the way of the Mahdi taking Khartoum, the rest of the Sudan and perhaps even Egypt. 49

Mr Gladstone, the Prime Minister, was speaking at a banquet given by the Lord Mayor of London when he made the announcement: 'We are about to withdraw – the order has been given – that withdrawal will include the *evacuation* of Cairo.' British troops would soon be coming home from Egypt, a year after they had landed to restore order. To keep them there any longer would mean added expense and trouble for the Government.

Then came the news of the massacre of Hicks's expedition. Worse was to follow: reports that another Egyptian army had been slaughtered, this time in the eastern Sudan, near Suakin. Desperately the Egyptian Government turned to their British advisers. They, in turn, informed the Cabinet in London. Gladstone did not want to become more involved than was necessary in Egypt. What was he to do? While the Mahdi's forces grew in strength the British ministers tried to put off making up their minds. Finally they decided to advise the Egyptians to give up the Sudan. The Egyptians at first would have none of this, but then they gave way. But how were they to do it? They would have to bring away their soldiers from all over the huge country. Who was to supervise this difficult task? There was not an officer in their army experienced enough to do it. One would have to be sent from England.

This is why General Charles Gordon came to be on the train to Dover that night in January 1884. Gordon was a most experienced soldier. After serving in the Crimean War as an officer in the Royal Engineers he had volunteered to fight in China when an uprising had broken out against the Emperor. It was known as the Taiping Rebellion. Gordon raised an army out of a disorderly mob of peasants – his 'Ever Victorious Army' he called them – and with them he succeeded in defeating the rebels. The Chinese Emperor rewarded him for this, and afterwards in Britain he was known as 'Chinese Gordon'. He had shown great courage and daring in facing the enemy with only a small cane in his hand. He had also shown that he could inspire respect and loyalty among very simple people.

General Gordon

Throughout his life Gordon demonstrated another quality. He was a very religious man. He spent many hours in prayer and read his Bible every day to give him guidance, which made him sure that he was working for God in all he did. This deep religious feeling carried him through many dangers in many parts of the world. He spent most of his life abroad. In fact he disliked living in England. He was therefore delighted when the Khedive Ismail made him Governor-General of the Sudan in 1877. Then he wholeheartedly tried to wipe out the hated slave trade. He made many enemies in the Sudan, but he also made many friends.

Towards the end of 1883 Gordon was back on one of his rare visits to England. Suddenly he found himself caught up in a newspaper campaign, urging the Government to do something to save the Sudan from the Mahdi. It was led by the famous journalist, W. T. Stead, editor of 'The Pall Mall Gazette'. Under a headline 'Chinese Gordon for the Sudan', Stead wrote: 51

We cannot send a regiment to Khartoum but we can send a man who on more than one occasion has proved himself more valuable in similar circumstances than an entire army. Why not send Chinese Gordon with full powers to Khartoum to assume absolute control of the territory, to treat with the Mahdi, to relieve the *garrisons*, and to do what he can to save what can be saved from the wreck of the Sudan?

Gordon, the popular hero, seemed the ideal choice: a brave and experienced soldier, who could obviously think for himself in a desperate situation, and who knew the Sudan at first-hand. Within a month he had been interviewed by members of the Cabinet, settled his affairs, and was off, with Colonel Stewart as his second-in-command.

The two men made their way from Dover to Calais, across France and Italy to Taranto, where they boarded the S.S. Tanjore for Port Said. In Cairo the Khedive reappointed Gordon as Governor-General of the Sudan, and Sir Evelyn Baring gave him last-minute instructions. By this time Gordon had given a lot of thought to the question of how the Sudan was to be ruled when Egyptian forces were withdrawn. He wanted the Khedive to appoint Zobeir Pasha. Although he was a former slave-trader and no friend of Gordon, he was a capable leader who had many followers. The two men could not agree, and so the matter remained unsettled when Gordon set off for Khartoum.

Gordon and Stewart made their way up country by train and river-boat, arriving in Khartoum in the middle of February, one month after leaving London. Here is a picture of Khartoum as it looked at this time. You are looking at it from the east. The river on the right of the picture is the Blue Nile, which here joins the main branch, or White Nile. Then, as now, it was by far the biggest town in the whole of the Sudan. There were about 50,000 people in it when Gordon arrived, many of them refugees from the Mahdi. About a hundred were Europeans, most of them Greeks. On the morning of 18 February they all turned out to welcome him and cheered as he made his way through

Khartoum, general view from the south-east

the narrow streets from the boat to the Governor's Palace (see the map on p. 55) overlooked the Blue Nile. That night the people set off fireworks and hung up coloured lights. After months of anxiety they knew that whatever happened they would be safe with General Gordon.

Soon after he arrived he began to move people out of the town. He sent about four hundred wounded soldiers down river, along with some women and children. He intended to remove all the Europeans and Egyptians as well as those Sudanese who wanted to go, leaving the rest to manage their own affairs. In letters and telegrams to London and Cairo he once again suggested that Zobeir might be appointed as some kind of ruler. The British Government, however, would not have a man who had been mixed up in the slave trade. Besides, they were annoyed that Gordon seemed to be more interested in the future of the Sudan than in evacuating the stranded garrisons. Slowly it began to dawn on them that Gordon might have no intention of abandoning the Sudan, but that he meant to hold out in Khartoum.

Right from the start of Gordon's mission there were serious misunderstandings between him and the Government in London. Some members thought that Gordon had been sent out only to report on the situation and to recommend how the Egyptian garrisons were to be removed. Gordon, of course, took it for granted that he was to carry out the evacuation himself. The longer he stayed in the Sudan, however, the more difficult he found it to abandon the people of Khartoum to their fate at the hands of the Mahdi.

Confusion between Khartoum and London increased. Gordon sent out messages by telegraph, sometimes up to a dozen in one day, pouring out ideas as they came into his head. Often he would contradict himself. Sometimes he was hopeful, sometimes he was in despair. One day he spoke about coming home, the next he was asking for troops to help him 'to smash up the Mahdi'. Ministers in London and Sir Evelyn Baring in Cairo did not know what to think. What was Gordon up to? Had he gone off his head? They were even more puzzled when, unknown to them for a while, the telegraph line from Khartoum was cut in March 1884. They were receiving only some of Gordon's messages and becoming impatient when he did not answer their urgent telegrams. It took them a long time to realise that Gordon was actually besieged in Khartoum and could not get out.

THE SIEGE OF KHARTOUM

Knowing that the Mahdi was bound to come some time, Gordon had begun to build up Khartoum's defences soon after he arrived. You will see from the map opposite that the town was defended on two sides by the River Nile and protected by several small forts, of which Omdurman was the strongest. It was guarded on the landward side by a mud wall. In front of the wall a deep ditch had been dug. In this he buried booby-traps made of broken bottles, spiked balls and biscuit tins filled with bullets, nails and gunpowder. All were tied to electric trip-wires. He kept constant watch on the river. Nine small steamers were converted into gunboats by covering them with

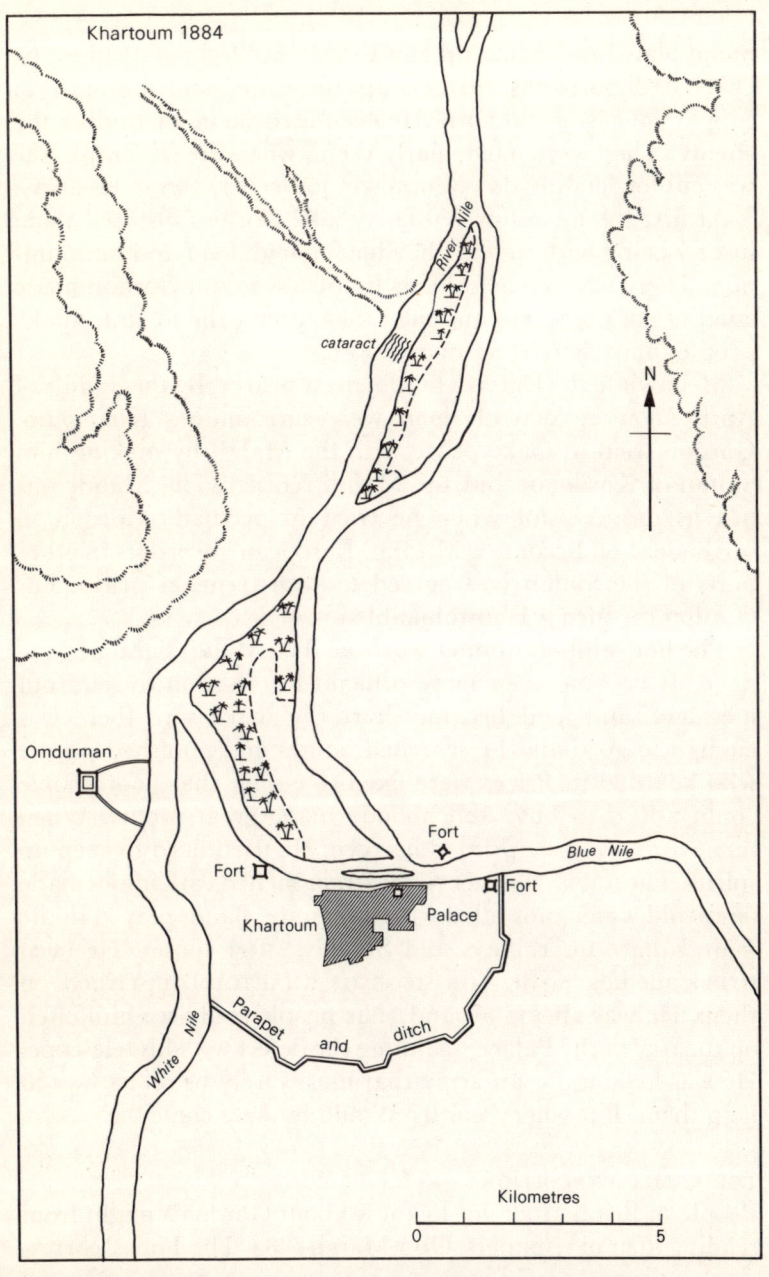

Khartoum 1884

River Nile

cataract

N

Omdurman

Fort

Fort

Blue Nile

Fort

Khartoum

Palace

White Nile

Parapet   and   ditch

Kilometres

0   5

metal plates and fitting up gun-turrets. With these steamers he evacuated garrisons further up the Nile, and brought in supplies of cattle and corn. He even used them for raiding the enemy. They were particularly useful when the telegraph line was cut for sending down messages to Berber, 200 miles away.

At first the townsfolk felt fairly safe. Gordon inspired them just by being with them. They had enough food and ammunition. There were 8,000 soldiers in the town, and Gordon made good use of them. He marched them about the town to make people think there were many more.

Meanwhile the Dervish hordes drew nearer. By the middle of April about 30,000 of them were surrounding Khartoum. Gordon tried to make peace with the Mahdi by making him Sultan of Kordofan, but the Mahdi refused. The Mahdi was just as unsuccessful when he tried to persuade Gordon to surrender and become a Muslim. European governors in other parts of the Sudan had agreed to such terms of peace. For Gordon the idea was unthinkable.

The hot, stifling summer wore on. The Mahdi tightened the siege. It became even more difficult for Gordon to send out messages, and food became short. To make sure there was enough to go round he searched houses and punished people who hoarded it. Prices were fixed to ensure that poor people could afford to buy, and nobody made great profits. When money ran short he printed his own. He tried hard to keep up spirits. The town's defences were strengthened with mines made out of old water cans filled with dynamite. Bands played in the main square on Fridays and Sundays after sunset. He even struck medals, with 'THE SIEGE OF KHARTOUM' inscribed on them. He was always around. The people could see him often on the roof of the Palace, scanning the desert with his telescope. He was looking for an army that must surely be on its way to help them. But where was it? Would it never come?

THE RELIEF EXPEDITION

People in Britain first got to know about Gordon's plight from reading their newspapers. On 1 March 1884 'The Times' correspondent in Khartoum reported: 'We are daily expecting British troops. We cannot bring ourselves to believe that we are abandoned by the British Government.'

Gladstone had never intended sending an army to relieve Gordon at Khartoum, but throughout the spring and summer people tried to make him change his mind. At public meetings, in letters to newspapers and by asking questions in Parliament friends of Gordon kept up a campaign for a relief expedition to be sent. It was unthinkable, they said, that their hero should have been sent out alone to face the dreaded Mahdi and his savage hordes and then abandoned. Queen Victoria expressed what many of her subjects were no doubt feeling when she said in a telegram to one of her ministers: 'General Gordon is in danger; you are bound to try and save him. . . . You have *incurred* fearful responsibility.' Prayers were said in churches and funds were raised to help General Gordon.

Gladstone's Cabinet as usual was divided as to what should be done. Gladstone and Lord Granville, the Foreign Secretary, thought nothing should be done. Gordon could get away any time he liked, they said. It was obvious he was only trying to force the Government to send out an army to conquer the Sudan. Throughout the summer, therefore, nothing was done to relieve Khartoum. Public opinion, meanwhile, mounted against the Government. People even made their own plans to save General Gordon. One scheme was for a party of a thousand sportsmen to fight their way to Khartoum. Finally an important member of the Cabinet threatened to resign if a relief force was not sent. Gladstone gave way. It was now August. The Prime Minister asked Parliament for a grant of £30,000 'to enable Her Majesty's Government to undertake operations for the relief of General Gordon should they become necessary, and to make certain preparations in respect thereof'. Notice that he seemed to be unconvinced that Gordon was in any danger.

Plans could now go forward to send an army to help Gordon. Its instructions were to bring Gordon and Stewart away from Khartoum and then withdraw. There was to be no question of the army being used to conquer the Sudan. Lord Wolseley was put in charge of the relief force. He was glad, because he had been badgering the Government to send an army for months. But it took weeks to decide how the expedition should be sent to Khartoum. Should it go all the way up the Nile, or would it be better to send it overland from Suakin on the Red Sea to Berber? This way was shorter, but a railway would have to be built to carry the men and their equipment across the scorching desert. Only when news came that Berber had been captured by the Mahdi was Wolseley's Nile route chosen.

To take a British army of 7,000 men and supplies 1,650 miles up the Nile called for a great deal of organisation. Nothing like it had been attempted since Napoleon's invasion of Russia in 1812. Thomas Cook & Son undertook to transport them by rail and steamer up the Nile as far as Wadi Halfa. To take the army farther up river Wolseley had arranged for boats to be built that were strong enough to stand up to the raging waters that surged round the dangerous *cataracts*. Boatmen had to be brought specially from Canada and West Africa to man them. A corps mounted on camels was another of Wolseley's bright ideas. This was to consist of eleven hundred of the best fighting

The relief expedition: towing the whalers through one of the cataracts on the Nile

The Relief Expedition: trouble with camels

men chosen from various regiments. They were to make the last stage of the journey to Khartoum by dashing across the desert to save time.

Early in September the Relief Expedition began to assemble in Egypt. It was made up entirely of British regiments brought from India, Malta, Gibraltar and bases at home. Once again many of the men were volunteers, soldiers who were bored with no fighting to do. The Prince of Wales tried again to go but his application was turned down by the Queen. More successful was a young military band-boy who stowed away to Egypt, because, as he said, he was the only member of the band without a medal.

The Expedition arrived at Wadi Halfa without a hitch, and soon before the end of the year a vast camp was set up. Mountains of stores were piled up, consisting of tins of corned beef, ships biscuits, lime juice, tea, pickles and compressed vegetables. Since Wolseley forbade the men to drink any alcohol he took out tons of sweets for them.

The Expedition began to run into trouble farther up river. Naval experts had confidently predicted that Wolseley would never get his boats through the nine miles of the Second Cataract. He proved them wrong. Thousands of local labourers pulled the boats over the rapids. The camels were troublesome, not easy to tame and very difficult to ride. Wolseley himself was thrown from one. All the time there was the terrible heat, sometimes as much as 60° Centigrade (140° Fahrenheit). The men were parched. There were no trees or grass in the country they were passing through, only bare grey rocks and sand.

While the Expedition slowly made its weary way up the Nile, Wolseley kept in touch with news from Khartoum. At Wadi Halfa he had heard of the death of Colonel Stewart. In trying to make his way down river in one of the steamers with some Europeans, Gordon's companion had landed and had been treacherously murdered. In November Wolseley received his first direct message from Gordon. 'We can hold out for forty days with ease,' wrote Gordon, 'after that it will be difficult.'

To speed his men on, Wolseley offered a prize of £100 for the battalion that reached Korti first. Here the Relief Force split in two. One party was to carry on by boat, while the other was to make its way on camels across the desert to the Nile at Metemma, a distance of 175 miles. Here, a hundred miles down river from Khartoum, Gordon's steamers were to pick them up.

Wolseley was still in his headquarters at Korti when on 30 December a runner came in from the desert with another message from Gordon. From a piece of paper the size of a postage stamp he read, 'Khartoum all right 12.12.84, C. G. Gordon.' This was just to deceive an enemy who might have captured the runner. He had a different story to tell. Supplies in Khartoum were desperately short. The Expedition would have to make all possible speed if it hoped to save Gordon now. The advance guard of the Desert Column had just started out to set up supply posts. The rest followed six days later, 1,600 men with 2,400 camels on the long trek to Metemma.

What happened next was a real test of endurance for the

Dervishes charging at Abu Klea

Camel Corps. One soldier wrote in his diary: 'Camels breaking down in all directions, and the native drivers are falling down and shrieking for water.' The soldiers almost died of thirst, too. With swollen tongues and cracked lips they longed for the wells at Abu Klea. Just as they were nearly there, on 16 January, they found their path was blocked. An army of 5,000 Dervishes stood ready for battle.

Next morning the exhausted British soldiers formed a battle square and wearily advanced. A savage battle followed. Frenzied Arab horsemen, wielding two-handed swords and lances six feet long, charged the British square. On and on they came. British rifles and machine-guns poured out orderly fire. When these jammed the men fought hand-to-hand from their barricade of crouching camels. Then the Dervishes drew back, leaving a thousand of their dead. The British lost under two hundred men. Fortunately for the British the enemy did not return that night, but the next afternoon they began to harass them all of the remaining twenty-three miles to the Nile. At last, the tired, sleepless, dishevelled force reached Metemma. Shortly afterwards they were aboard four of Gordon's little steamers.

61

The captain of one of the steamers handed the British commander a cloth bag. Inside were the last of Gordon's diaries. Throughout the siege he wrote down what he thought about the events all around him. He had sent down earlier instalments already. Eagerly the British commander read the diaries. They told how the Mahdi had moved up his heavy guns and from the end of September had begun to bombard Khartoum. All the while Gordon had only the vaguest idea of what was happening outside. He had obviously learnt about Stewart's death, but had no notion how far away the Relief Force was. He apparently expected it to be coming any day. The last entry was dated 13 December and read:

> Now mark this, if the Expeditionary Force, and I ask for no more than ten thousand men, does not come in ten days the town may fall; and I have done my best for the honour of my country. Good-bye. C. G. Gordon.
> You send me no information, though you have lots of money.
>
> C.G.G.

It was now 21 January.

The British now knew that if they were to save Gordon every moment counted. But it took three days to fit the ships out for the journey up to Khartoum. The soldiers sailed in two of them, the 'Bordein' and the 'Tel Helwein'. Two days later the 'Bordein' struck a rock and they had to stop and repair the damage. More time was lost when supplies of firewood ran out and they had to go ashore to collect more. By this time some of the ships' crews were ready to go over to the Mahdi. At last Khartoum was in sight. Then suddenly some Dervishes opened fire from the shore. Gordon was dead, they shouted. Were they bluffing? Was Gordon still alive?

On the morning of 28 January the steamers reached Khartoum. The help that Gordon had longed and prayed for since the previous March had finally come. But no flag was flying from the roof of the Governor's Palace. The Relief Force had arrived two days late.

The two steamers trying to rescue Gordon at Khartoum

We shall probably never know exactly what happened during Gordon's last weeks at Khartoum. He left no account of what he did. At least none has been found. Historians have had to piece together the reports of other people who survived the siege. It seems that the Mahdi finally decided to attack Khartoum as revenge for the defeat of his men at Abu Klea by the Relief Force. Having stormed and taken the fort at Omdurman he now had command of all the approaches to the stricken town. The people were starving. Food was so scarce that they had to eat dogs, cats, monkeys, and even rats and raw *gum*. Many crept out at night and joined the Mahdi. Hundreds of dead bodies lay about the streets. The stench was sickening. Yet Gordon himself seemed to be as fearless as ever. He was still to be seen walking among the people telling them that help was at hand and assuring them that he would never leave them.

Before dawn on 26 January the Mahdi launched his final assault. From his camp on the west bank of the White Nile, about 50,000 of his men stole over to the other side under cover of darkness. Stealthily they landed on a stretch of beach that

63

the low water of the river had recently left exposed, and which Gordon's men were too weak to defend. In no time at all the Dervishes were all over the battle-scarred town. Resistance was hopeless. With wild shouts they made for Gordon's palace. Inside the grounds they held back for fear of buried mines.

Dawn was just rising when Gordon appeared at the top of the stairs. He was in dress uniform and armed with a sword and pistol. The Dervishes paused and were quiet. Then some bolder than the rest pushed forward. One called out, 'O cursed one, your time has come.' There was a rush of spears and Gordon fell dead. Later one of the Mahdi's European prisoners saw some Dervishes carrying something in a blood-stained cloth. It was Gordon's severed head.

For two days Khartoum was wrecked and *pillaged*. Men, women and children were butchered or taken away as slaves.

The men of the Relief Force knew nothing of all this as they drew nearer Khartoum. All they saw was a smouldering, deserted town. They knew there was nothing more to do, and so under heavy gunfire from the shore they sailed back to Metemma. With the greatest luck they survived the wreck of both steamers and landed.

NATIONAL HERO

All Britain went into deep mourning for General Gordon. Services were said in churches and his picture, edged with black, was displayed in many houses and shops. Everybody was shocked at the news of his death. Newspapers had been confidently reporting the Relief Force's progress for weeks. Why had they failed to save Gordon? What had gone wrong? Who was to blame? There was only one answer. Like many of her subjects, Queen Victoria blamed Gladstone. In plain language, not in code, she sent a telegram to him. It read:

These news from Khartoum are frightful, and to think that all this might have been prevented and many precious lives saved by earlier action is too frightful.

An artist imagines what Gordon's last stand in the Governor's Palace, Khartoum, was like.

Angry letters appeared in the newspapers. Why had there been such a delay in sending the Relief Force in the first place? In Parliament members of the Government had a hard job explaining what had happened. Gladstone became even more unpopular. His enemies said that instead of being 'G.O.M.' – initials for 'Grand Old Man' – he should be known as 'M.O.G.' – 'Murderer of Gordon'. Wherever he went he was hooted and jeered at. When next they got the chance to vote in a General Election many people, remembering the death of Gordon, voted against him in 1886. Meanwhile throughout the spring of 1885 everybody blamed everyone else for bungling the whole business. To please the enraged public, Gladstone finally with reluctance promised to 'smash the Mahdi' as a way of avenging Gordon's death. But in a few weeks' time there was risk of a war with Russia. This was a good excuse for taking British troops away from the Sudan altogether. The soldiers were not sorry to leave! They had suffered many losses and had no heart to stay on. Soon the storm of anger in Britain died down.

Now that he was dead General Gordon became even more of a national hero. Statues were put up in his honour and countless books were written about him. For thousands of people he was a perfect example of a brave, God-fearing, Christian soldier who had died in a noble cause. The years passed and a new generation grew up that liked to question old beliefs. In 1919 a very witty and clever writer, named Lytton Strachey, published a book called 'Eminent Victorians'. Gordon was the subject of one of his essays. In it Strachey showed Gordon as a drunkard and a *hypocrite*. Many young people were amused. Older people were shocked. Since then writers have shown that Strachey was wrong. Gordon was, in fact, a brave soldier who did not drink more than most. Yet there still remain many questions about Gordon that are puzzling. He could have got away from Khartoum any time he liked until the very end. Did Gordon actually choose to die in Khartoum? Is this why he accepted the job in the first place? We may never know the answer but it is interesting to ask all the same.

7 Kitchener and the Re-conquest of the Sudan

In 1892 an Englishman named Alfred Milner published a book entitled 'England in Egypt'. In it he wrote:

> It is not a pleasant reflection that the former dominions of Egypt in the Sudan, are, perhaps, the only portion of the world where civilisation has, during the fifteen years preceding 1892, distinctly *retrograded* – the one region deliberately given back to barbarism. . . . Frightful – indeed almost incredible are the ravages which war, *pestilence*, and famine in their most hideous forms, have *wrought* during the past ten years in the Upper Valley of the Nile. It is estimated that more than half of the population have perished.

'England in Egypt' was an important book because it made many people in Britain interested in the Sudan again.

When British forces were withdrawn from the Sudan, Egyptian garrisons in the more remote parts of the country either gave in or were wiped out. The Mahdi and his followers could now do as they liked. It was just about this time, in the summer of 1885, that the Mahdi died. He was succeeded by one of his chief followers, the *Khalifa* Abdullah. To people in Britain he was nothing but a cruel tyrant. Cruel he may have been, but to the people of the Sudan he was a very conscientious and powerful ruler. He made Omdurman his capital and built a magnificent tomb in which rested the remains of the Mahdi. With his armies he tried to wipe out all resistance to his authority and bring together the peoples of the Sudan under his leadership. These were indeed terrible years for the Sudan, with warfare, disease and famine. To Englishmen like Alfred Milner the Sudan under the Khalifa was a very barbarous place indeed.

People who read Milner's book were shocked at what they read. It made them think again of General Gordon and they were ashamed to think that he had died in vain. They became indignant that gallant British soldiers had been defeated by what they took to be ignorant savages.

The British Government's interest in the Sudan was aroused again, too. The Prime Minister for most of the twenty years after 1885 was an elderly-looking nobleman called Lord Salisbury, who was Foreign Secretary as well, because he was particularly interested in foreign affairs. He believed that the British should hold on to Egypt. Gladstone had always intended that British troops should be withdrawn from Egypt and had only been prevented from arranging this by the events leading up to the death of Gordon. Salisbury thought that Egypt could be used as a base for the British to protect their sea route to India by way of the Suez Canal. In the past the British had

Lord Salisbury

depended on their influence in Turkey; recently they had been losing their power there. Egypt, to Lord Salisbury, was therefore vital to Britain's security.

This meant that Egypt would have to be safe from attack, and so the British Government began to think about reconquering at least parts of the Sudan. Salisbury realised that this would mean a lot of fighting and a great deal of expense. He knew also that British taxpayers would not want to pay for a war which to them was not absolutely necessary. It is true that Britain was prosperous, but people still remembered those disastrous campaigns in the Sudan of the 1880s. Salisbury would have to proceed very cautiously if the Sudan was to be re-conquered. The cost would have to be paid by Egypt.

It so happened that Egypt under British control was wealthier than it had ever been before. What is more, under its British officers, the Egyptian Army had recovered the confidence it had lost under Arabi. From their bases at Suakin and Wadi Halfa the Egyptians had been able to hold back the Khalifa's forces and even defeat them in battle. Egypt, with its full treasury and confident soldiers, would be able to provide men and money for the re-conquest of the Sudan.

IMPERIALISM

Even without the British Government's plans there was little chance that the Sudan would be left alone for long. If the British did not take it over, other Europeans would. During the last twenty years of the nineteenth century people in Europe became very interested in the other continents of the world. In Central Asia, China, Indo-China and especially Africa, they saw the chance to take over countries that were too weak to stand up for themselves.

In Africa, as we have seen, the French in Tunisia and the British in Egypt, had started in the 1880s. Governments of other countries, such as Portugal, Belgium, Italy and Germany, joined in. Rapidly they staked out claims for themselves to huge tracts of jungle, bush and desert in other parts of the continent. The 'Scramble for Africa' was on. You will see what each country took over the page. All this land-grabbing might easily

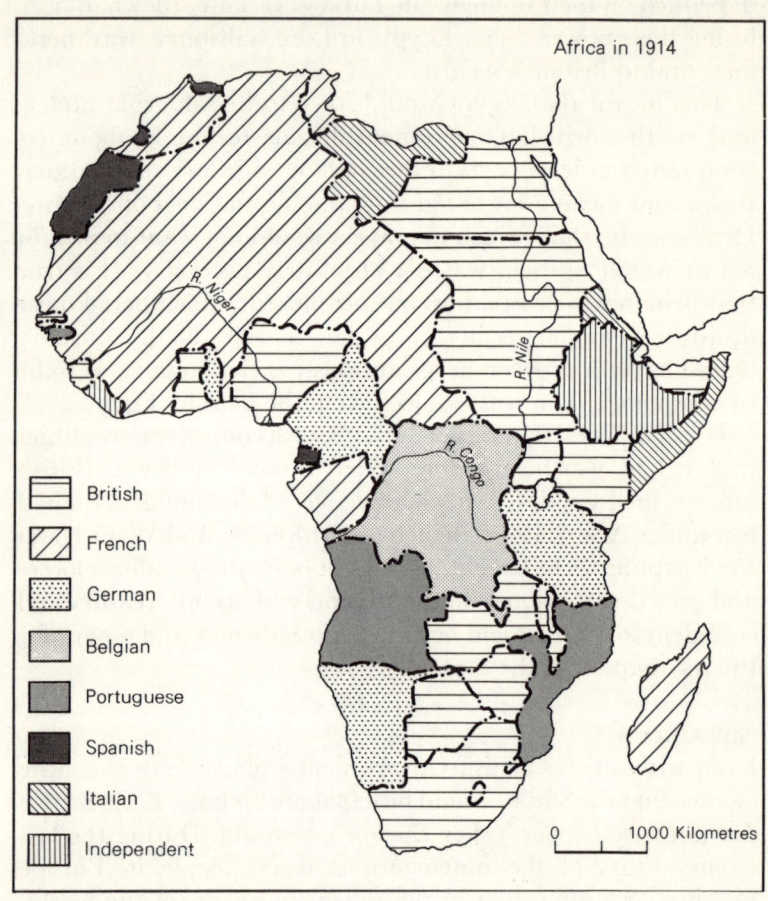

Africa in 1914

British
French
German
Belgian
Portuguese
Spanish
Italian
Independent

R. Niger

R. Congo

R. Nile

0   1000 Kilometres

have led to war if the statesmen of Europe had not worked together to prevent it. For instance, at a conference held at Berlin in 1884, they agreed to divide up West Africa and the basin of the Congo.

Africa was explored about this time by men such as David Livingstone and H. M. Stanley. Traders followed in their wake, eager to make profits by exploiting the natural wealth of the 'Dark Continent'. Missionaries came to put down slavery and convert the heathen. Engineers cut their way through the continent with roads and railways. Towns sprang up. In

London, Paris, Berlin and Brussels financiers saw opportunities of making new fortunes. They invested money in trading companies, including the Royal Niger Company and the British East African Company. Huge profits were made. And so by the 1890s people in Europe were becoming very proud of their growing empires overseas.

The native peoples of Africa had no say in what was happening to their continent. By the end of the nineteenth century there were hardly any independent African states left. Kings and chiefs had signed treaties, often without understanding them, by which a trading company or a government took away their land or made it into a 'protectorate', which was a kind of colony in which the local ruler was allowed to go on ruling. Sometimes these rulers resisted and troops had to be brought out from Europe to 'restore order'. We have seen how this was done in Egypt. The word that is given to this extension of European power over peoples in other parts of the world at this time is Imperialism.

By the early 1890s Europeans were particularly interested in East Africa. This alarmed the British. They thought the French and the Germans, in pushing their way inland from their colonies on the coast, might try to gain control of the headwaters of the Nile, which were vital for the welfare of Egypt. This was another reason why the Sudan now became specially important to Britain. Lord Salisbury determined to keep the French and Germans out. He signed a treaty with the Germans in 1890; they agreed to take over Tanganyika, the mainland part of what is now Tanzania, while the British got Kenya and Uganda. The French, meanwhile, were persuaded to develop their colonies in West Africa. This did not stop them from resenting the British control of Egypt, as we shall see later in this chapter.

The Italians were busy in East Africa too. They wanted to enlarge their colony on the Red Sea coast at Massawa. But they were never as powerful as the French and Germans and so less dangerous to the British. In fact they were very useful to the British, for they took away the Khalifa's attention from the

71

borders of Egypt. The Italians wanted to conquer Ethiopia. It was here in a battle at Adowa that an Italian army was defeated in 1896. This was a great blow to Italians' pride, a European army cut down by people they regarded as ignorant, backward savages. More important for the British, they could no longer count on the Italians to keep the Khalifa diverted from Egypt. He might be able to threaten the British there.

Lord Salisbury now saw he had an excuse for re-conquering the Sudan. People in Britain could be persuaded that they would be supporting Italy, a friendly country, and fighting for European civilisation against barbarous Africans. Most saw the campaign as a welcome revenge for the death of General Gordon.

KITCHENER

The British laid their plans for the Sudan campaign with great care. They had to pay for most of it themselves, however. This was because the Russians and French, who were no friends of Britain at this time, instructed their members of the Caisse de la Dette (that international body which still supervised Egyptian finances) to prevent the costs being paid by Egypt.

The leader of the expedition was the Sirdar, or Commander-in-Chief of the Egyptian Army, General Sir Herbert Kitchener. In many ways he was ideally suited for the task. He was only forty-five, and had spent most of his life as a soldier in the *Middle East*. He spoke Arabic fluently, and in Gordon's time he had acted as a go-between in the desert, dressed in Arab clothes, passing on messages from Khartoum to Cairo. Gordon thought so highly of him that he wrote in his diary: 'If Kitchener would take the place he would be the best man to put in as governor-general.' Kitchener was most eager to avenge Gordon's death. As a soldier he was regarded as very conscientious and painstaking rather than brilliant. He got on very well with Lord Salisbury. Other politicians like him too. This was because he kept down expenses. He economised on everything such as clothing, pay and allowances. He even cut down on medical supplies. This made him very unpopular with his men, but

Sir Herbert Kitchener

Kitchener did not care. In appearance he was very tall and erect and always very stiff and aloof. He never spoke to a common soldier if he could possibly help it. Yet the men respected him, and drill instructors paid him the greatest compliment, by growing their moustaches to look like his.

OMDURMAN
Early in June 1896 a fleet of pleasure-steamers supplied by Thomas Cook & Son began to transport the Egyptian expeditionary force of 10,000 men up the Nile to Wadi Halfa. There was no hurry. At Wadi Halfa a railway was started, and from there men and supplies were brought on by rail as soon as stretches of track were completed. The Dervishes fought hard in several battles, but the expedition made good progress, despite sandstorms, torrential rain and a serious outbreak of *cholera.*

Because many people at home said that the campaign was a waste of money, Lord Salisbury had originally ordered Kitchener to go only as far as Dongola. But Kitchener was determined to press on to Khartoum and conquer the whole of the Sudan. He would need more men to do this because the Khalifa's resistance got stronger the further south they went. Kitchener therefore left the expedition and sailed back to Britain. He went the rounds of influential people to get their support for his request that British troops should be sent out to help him. It was the summer of 1897. London was full of people celebrating Queen Victoria's *Diamond Jubilee*–'Sixty Glorious Years' on the throne. Crowds gathered to watch the soldiers of the Queen marching past in procession, men from different parts of the vast British Empire. How proud people were of this Empire! They were just in the mood for adding to it, and so Kitchener got the men he wanted.

The British *reinforcements* consisted of an infantry *division*, a brigade of artillery and the 21st Lancers, a dashing cavalry regiment. One of its officers was a young man of only twenty-three, who had volunteered specially to fight in the Sudan. His name was Winston Churchill. This was the same Winston Churchill who as Prime Minister led Britain in the Second World War. When the Sudan campaign opened he was serving with another regiment on the North-West Frontier of India. All was quiet in India at this time, however, and Churchill was bored. He longed for action and the chance to make a name for himself, so he applied to be *seconded* to Kitchener's forces in the Sudan. Since he was the grandson of a duke and knew many influential people in England, including the Prime Minister himself, he had little trouble in getting posted to Egypt. There was one condition laid down: he would have to take three months' leave and serve without pay. This was a blow. He was already very hard up and in debt, so he had to go to the Sudan as war correspondent for the 'Morning Post' of London, which agreed to pay him £15 for every column of *dispatch* that was printed.

74   Churchill later wrote a book about his experiences in the

*The young
Winston
Churchill*

Sudan, entitled 'The River War'. In it he tells how he joined
Kitchener's army at the end of August after it had made its way
up the Nile to within a few miles of the Khalifa's capital of
Omdurman. The British and Egyptians had already beaten the
Dervishes in battle several times, notably at the Atbara, in
which they had gone into fight to the sounds of Scottish bag-
pipes and English military bands, and shouting 'Remember
Gordon!' Now they were within striking distance of the Khalifa's
army gathered in front of Omdurman.

A great battle was about to be fought. This is how Churchill
describes the British and Egyptian armies on the march, as he
saw them from a hill not far from the Nile:

> The sun had just risen, and the atmosphere was clear. A
> wonderful spectacle was displayed. The grand army of the
> Nile marched towards its goal: a long row of great brown
> masses of infantry and artillery, with a fringe of cavalry
> dotting the plain for miles in front, with the Camel Corps –

75

chocolate-coloured men on cream-coloured camels—
stretching into the desert on the right, and the white gunboats stealing silently up the river on the left, *scrutinising* the
banks with their guns. Far in the rear the transport trailed
away into the *mirage*, and far in front the field-glass dis-
closed the enemy's patrols.

The next day, 1 September, while out on *reconnaissance*, he
spotted the Khalifa's army:

Then four miles away on our right front, I *perceived* a long
line with white spots. It was the enemy. It seemed to us, as
we looked, that there might be 3,000 men behind a high
dense *zeriba* of thorn bushes. Suddenly the whole black line

*On patrol
in the Sudan*

began to move. It was made of men, not bushes. Behind it
other immense masses and lines of men appeared over the
crest; and while we watched, amazed by the wonder of the
sight, the whole face of the slope became black with swarm-
ing savages. Four miles from end to end, and as it seemed in
five great divisions, this mighty army advanced—swiftly!

The Khalifa's army was in fact 60,000 strong!

Meanwhile British gunboats began to shell Omdurman.
Huge holes were torn in the town's walls, and the white dome of
the Mahdi's tomb was sent crashing to the ground.

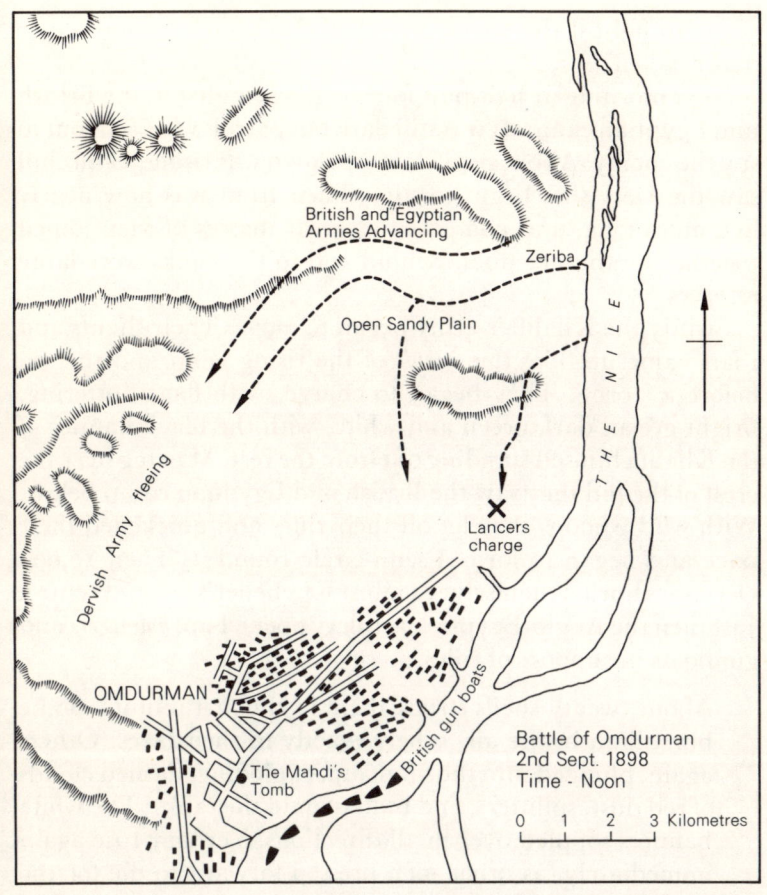

British and Egyptian
Armies Advancing

Zeriba

Open Sandy Plain

THE NILE

Dervish Army fleeing

×
Lancers
charge

OMDURMAN

The Mahdi's
Tomb

British gun boats

Battle of Omdurman
2nd Sept. 1898
Time – Noon

0   1   2   3 Kilometres

Both armies took up positions on what Churchill described
as 'a wide, rolling, sandy plain of great extent, surrounded on
three sides by rocky hills and ridges, and patched with coarse,
starveling grass or occasional bushes.' Five miles separated the
armies: the Dervishes on the higher ground, the British and
Egyptians – six brigades drawn up in crescent formation – with
their backs to the Nile.

No fighting took place that day. The Khalifa's men halted
and Kitchener's set up camp behind a barricade of thornbush,

ready to fight if the enemy attacked. No attack came even as darkness fell.

Next morning at half-past four bugles sounded in the British and Egyptian camp. It was still dark but patrols were sent out to spy the enemy. About six o'clock, as dawn was rising, Churchill saw the Dervishes begin to stir: 'Their front was now nearly five miles long, and composed of great masses of men joined together by thinner lines. Behind and to the flanks were large reserves.'

Swiftly the Khalifa's army began to move. Their shouts and roars came up 'like the *tumult* of the rising wind and the sea before a storm'. They began to charge, with flags fluttering, bright green, dark green and white, with the black banner of the Khalifa himself standing out from the rest. Massing over the crest of the hill they saw the British and Egyptian camp below. With wild whoops they let off their rifles and quickened their pace and began to form a semi-circle round it. Then 10,000 Dervishes hurled themselves against Kitchener's left and centre. Just then the Anglo-Egyptian artillery opened up, *howitzers* and gunboats in support of rifles.

> About twenty shells struck them in the first minute. Some burst high in the air, others exactly in their faces. Others again, plunged into the sand and, exploding, dashed clouds of red dust, splinters, and bullets amid the ranks. The white banners toppled over in all directions. Yet they rose again immediately, as other men pressed forward to die for the Mahdi's sacred cause.

The survivors retreated, leaving some 2,000 dead: the first wave of the Dervish attack had been repulsed. A flanking attack on Kitchener's camel corps was also thrown back.

Now the order went out to advance on Omdurman. Kitchener wanted to take the town before nightfall and so avoid street fighting. Churchill's Lancers went off to *reconnoitre* and clear the way for the rest of the army following behind. Suddenly they came across some Dervishes in the dried-up bed of a river. They charged and there was some fierce fighting at close quarters.

The charge of the 21st Lancers at Omdurman

British casualties were heavy and later three Victoria Crosses were awarded. Churchill wrote at length about this charge, but it had little real effect on the course of the battle.

As the Anglo-Egyptian army moved up, the Khalifa, with the main body of his men, charged from the west. Kitchener's handling of this, the second phase of the battle, was masterly. Coolly he ordered his brigades to turn and meet the attack on different flanks as if they were going through drill movements on the parade ground. With deadly skill they were able to train their superior firing power on the hordes of horsemen. Thus the second attack was stopped. Then a fresh wave of Dervishes swooped on them, but these, too, were mown down. The enemy was routed. By half past eleven Kitchener was remarking that they had had 'a thorough dusting'. After a short rest in the middle of the day the British and Egyptian forces were ready to march on to the Khalifa's capital.

Thus ended the battle of Omdurman. Once again a small British force–8,200 with 17,600 Egyptians and Sudanese–had been able to defeat a much larger native army. Of course, the British side had much better weapons, including the most modern and deadly artillery. The Khalifa's men had only spears and old-fashioned rifles. Kitchener lost under five hundred men in casualties. On the Dervish side the slaughter was colossal. The British killed off many of the wounded and prisoners. Over 11,000 stinking, swollen corpses had to be picked up from the battlefield and buried. Everybody thought the Dervishes had fought bravely. The popular poet of the time, Rudyard Kipling, published a poem, called 'Fuzzy-Wuzzy', the name given to the curly-haired warriors of the Sudan. One of the verses ran like this:

So 'ere's to you, Fuzzy-Wuzzy, at your 'ome in the Sudan;
You're a pore *benighted* 'eathen but a first-class fightin' man;
An' 'ere's to you, Fuzzy-Wuzzy, with your 'ayrick 'ead of 'air—
You big black boundin' beggar—for you broke a British square!

Omdurman was quickly handed over to Kitchener. The Khalifa himself had already fled. A year later he was hunted down and killed. Meanwhile the Mahdi's tomb was completely demolished. His corpse was taken and thrown into the Nile, his skull being taken back to Egypt. Winston Churchill was one of the people who were shocked at this treatment of the remains of one who was regarded by many as a holy man. As a result of their protests the Mahdi's skull was later brought back and buried in the Sudan.

Three days after the battle of Omdurman a service of remembrance was held over the river at Khartoum, near the spot where General Gordon had been killed thirteen years before. The British and Egyptian flags were hoisted and Gordon's favourite hymn, 'Abide with me', was sung. To everyone's surprise Kitchener shook with sobs and was so moved that someone else had to dismiss the parade. On hearing the news of the ceremony Queen Victoria wrote in her diary, 'Surely, he is avenged!'

FASHODA

Kitchener now opened sealed orders he had received from the Prime Minister. He was to go south from Khartoum on a most important mission. Two years before, a party of Frenchmen, led by a certain Major Marchand, was known to have left Brazzaville, a town on the Congo, to make its way across Africa to link up with a similar party coming from Ethiopia. They were supposed to meet on the headwaters of the Nile at a little village called Fashoda. Kitchener was ordered to find out what they were doing.

News reached Khartoum that the French had in fact been at Fashoda for six weeks. With a fleet of five gunboats Kitchener set off at the head of two companies of Cameron Highlanders, a couple of battalions of Sudanese and a battery of artillery.

For the next few weeks the world waited for news. Far up the Nile, the representatives of two of the most powerful countries in the world would face each other. The fate of thousands of square miles of Africa would be decided by two men. But the telegraph line went no farther south than Khartoum, and Kitchener, who hated reporters, took none along with him. What was going to happen next?

A memorial to Major Marchand in Paris, showing the route of his expedition

Kitchener's *flotilla* arrived at Fashoda after a fortnight's journey on 18 September. Major Marchand was there all right. With his eight officers and 120 West Africans, he had made his way across hundreds of miles of desert, jungle and swamp—some of the most difficult country in the world. They had had a small steam launch, but it had to be taken to pieces and carried part of the way. They had reached their goal, however. They had set up camp at Fashoda, raised the French flag and taken over all the land round about in the name of France. Unfortunately the party from Ethiopia had arrived at Fashoda before them but had not waited.

Kitchener and Marchand met and took an instant liking to each other. Kitchener entertained Marchand on his boat, but he was most tactful. He spoke fluent French, he wore his Egyptian instead of his British uniform and flew the Egyptian flag to spare the Frenchman's feelings. Yet very politely and firmly he told Marchand that the French were trespassing on land that belonged to Egypt. Marchand must pull down his flag and leave. Just as politely Marchand insisted that by agreement with a local ruler this land was now French. If Kitchener tried to remove him he would resist. He could not go unless ordered to leave by his Government. Each having stated his case, the two men parted on good terms. After pitching camp farther up the Nile, Kitchener left a force to keep an eye on the French, then sailed down to Khartoum and went back to England.

By the time Kitchener reached home in October, everybody knew about the meeting at Fashoda. Newspapers in Britain and France were full of *lurid* stories about ministers and ambassadors having hurried meetings and making fiery speeches. Each country accused the other of trespassing on its territory. Britain and France seemed to be on the brink of war.

The British saw Marchand's mission as a brave but spiteful attempt to rob them of what they saw as a richly deserved prize, the whole of the Sudan. In France people said that the British had no right to the Sudan and that the Egyptians had long since abandoned it. Marchand had therefore every right to claim part of it for France. Besides, who had reached Fashoda first? How typical it was of the British to bully Marchand and try to push him out! But Frenchmen would not be bullied. To demand Marchand's withdrawal, said the French Foreign Minister, was an insult to France's national honour. France would resist!

The British Government remained firm and cool amid all the hullabaloo in the newspapers. Lord Salisbury wanted to avoid war with France, but was determined that Marchand should be turned out. To him Marchand was merely 'an explorer in difficulties upon the Upper Nile'. There was no question about it. The whole of the Sudan belonged to Egypt and to Britain by right of conquest.

War did not break out over Fashoda after all. From the start the British had the upper hand. They had an army in the Sudan; Marchand had only a handful of men. The British Government was united, the French had many troubles at home to deal with. France had no ally willing to take on the Royal Navy, and was not strong enough to fight Britain alone. Major Marchand was therefore ordered by the French Government to withdraw from Fashoda.

Kitchener had arrived in England by the time news of this broke. At Dover he was greeted with a band playing 'See! the conquering hero comes!' Crowds cheered him on the special train that took him to London to receive the freedom of the City. As for Major Marchand, he did as he was told and was escorted down the Nile to Cairo and home. The rest of the French left in December. They must have thought that their mission was a waste of time and that their Government had let them down.

THE ANGLO-EGYPTIAN SUDAN

With the threat of war with France over, people now asked if all the fuss had been necessary. If the French had been allowed to stay on at Fashoda would they have been able to do Britain any harm? The country itself was of little value, except to the local tribesmen; and as for trying to dam the Nile to cut off Egypt's water supply, why there was not any stone for miles!   83

The land was all swampy. But the excitement over Fashoda had at least one good result. It led to the Governments of Britain and France coming to an agreement in 1899 about the Sudan. The French said that they would stay out of the Nile Valley and allow the British to have a free hand there. In return France got more territory farther west. From then on the name of Fashoda disappeared and the place was renamed Kodok.

In the same year an agreement was made between Britain and Egypt. The Sudan was by now firmly under British control, but how was it to be run? The campaign had cost over £2¼ million, most of which had been paid by Egypt. Much of the fighting, however, had been done by the British. It was agreed, therefore, that the Sudan should belong to both countries, and so for the next fifty years or so it was known as the Anglo-Egyptian Sudan. Both Governments were responsible for ruling it, which is why this arrangement is known as a condominium. In fact, of course, the Sudan was run by the British with some Egyptian help. The British appointed the Governor-general, though he was supposed to rule in the name of the Khedive. As you might expect, the first Governor-General was Kitchener, now known as Lord Kitchener of Khartoum. Though he made many enemies he was a firm ruler. One of the first things he did was to set up a school in Khartoum to train young Sudanese to run their own country. He called it Gordon College. It became the University of Khartoum in 1956, the year in which the Sudan became an independent country.

8 Egypt under Lord Cromer

LORD CROMER

Kitchener's spectacular conquest of the Sudan would never have been possible if it had not been for a rather serious, prim-looking man, who worked at a desk in his office a thousand miles away in Cairo. This was Lord Cromer, British Agent and Consul-General in Egypt. Officially he was no more than Britain's representative. In fact he had more power than the Khedive himself. Winston Churchill once met Cromer with the Khedive Abbas, then a young man about Churchill's own age, and wrote: 'The Khedive's attitude reminded me of a schoolboy who is brought to see another schoolboy in the presence of the headmaster.' Though he always treated the Khedive with the greatest respect, there was no mistaking that Cromer was the real ruler of Egypt.

Sir Evelyn Baring, Lord Cromer

Cromer took up his appointment in 1883, the year after the start of the British occupation. He was then known as Sir Evelyn Baring. Earlier he had served for three years as one of the two Controllers of the Caisse de la Dette. For the next three years he was a member of the Viceroy's Council in India. He was brought back to Egypt because he knew so much about the country's finances, and seemed to be the only person capable of sorting them out. He was a very cautious, thorough and painstaking man.

Lord Cromer came from a rich family of bankers and was born at Cromer Hall in Norfolk in 1841. After his father's death he was brought up by his mother who was a very learned woman. She believed that her son should be able to look after himself. At the age of twelve he was left to find his own way home to England from Salzburg in Austria. He trained as an officer in the Royal Engineers and rose to the rank of Major. He served in many parts of the British Empire before taking up his appointment in Egypt. In India people called him 'Over-Baring', which gives you an idea of his character. In Egypt he was known as 'le Grand *Ours*' or simply 'the Lord'.

THE MIRACLE OF EGYPT

In his memoirs Lord Cromer later wrote that he returned to Egypt in 1883 with the ambition of 'leading the Egyptian people from bankruptcy to *solvency* and then onward to *affluence*, from Khedivial *monstrosities* to British justice, and from oriental methods *veneered* with a *spurious* European civilisation towards the true civilisation of the West, based on the principles of the Christian moral code'. Do you understand what he meant? If you don't, look up the difficult words in the glossary.

His first task was to bring some order into Egypt's financial affairs. Every year millions of pounds had to be paid out not only to the European bondholders who had lent money to the Khedive Ismail before he went bankrupt, but also to those people whose property had been lost or damaged during the riots in Alexandria and the bombardment by the British in 1882. Cromer made sure that this money was paid, but within five years the Egyptian Government was actually earning more money than it was spending. This was largely as a result of careful account-keeping. After twenty years Egypt's finances were among the soundest and best run in the world.

The 'miracle' of Egypt that Cromer worked came from saving money, but it was due also to making money. Cromer helped to make Egypt prosperous again. Vast areas of the Delta were made to grow crops. The old *barrage* across the Nile north of Cairo, built by French engineers forty years before, was repaired and raised. Water could be stored from the annual flood and then released in the dry season. By this *perennial* irrigation farmers had enough water for two, and sometimes even three crops, to be grown one after the other in the same ground during one year. British engineers, led by Sir Colin Scott-Moncrieff, were largely responsible for this work. They were brought from India, where they had carried out similar schemes on rivers there. The working conditions for Egyptian labourers were improved: forced labour by means of the detested courbash was abolished. As a result of these improvements, exports of cotton and sugar were trebled within ten years.

The Aswan Dam soon after it was opened

Visitors could not help noticing Egypt's new prosperity. In 1905 a Frenchman noted how ships off Alexandria, after trying in vain to unload their cargoes, had to move on to another port because the harbour was so crowded. The harbour could not be extended fast enough to cope with the increased trade. Cairo, he said, had been transformed 'as if touched by a magic wand'.

One of the greatest engineering projects of the age was the Aswan Dam. Far up the Nile a wall, eighty-four feet high and a quarter of a mile long, was built under the direction of Sir John Aird. It took six years to complete and cost £2 million, which was raised by Lord Cromer's friends among the bankers and financiers of Europe. It was opened in 1902. As a result about half a million acres of parched desert – the size of a county in Britain like Berkshire or Lanarkshire – could be used for cultivation all year round, with the water stored in the reservoir behind the dam.

Cromer made other modern improvements too. As a result of proper sanitation in towns and the introduction of better health services, there were fewer outbreaks of dangerous diseases like cholera. Altogether, with more food for people to eat, more work and better health, the population rose from under 7 million in 1882, to nearly 10 million in 1897. Other changes were also made in the law courts, the police and in education. The army was modernised too, and we have seen already how useful it was in the re-conquest of the Sudan under Kitchener.

FOREIGN INTERFERENCE

Although the British made many changes in Egypt they could never do what they liked there. Egypt was never a British colony. It was only under British military occupation, and this was intended to be temporary. Strictly speaking, Egypt belonged to Turkey; the Sultan was still the Khedive's overlord. In 1887 the British tried to make an agreement with the Sultan; they said they would take out all their troops from Egypt

within three years, provided that all was quiet and orderly in the country. This was known as the Drummond Wolff *Convention*, after Sir Henry Drummond Wolff, the British representative in Turkey. The Sultan would not agree, however, partly because of French and Russian interference. And so after that the British did not pay much attention to Turkey's rights in Egypt, and the Sultan did not interfere with what the British did.

Other governments did interfere, but they were perfectly within their rights. All foreigners in Egypt came under regulations that were known as the Capitulations. These were ancient privileges originally granted by the Sultan to protect Europeans in his empire from Muslim laws against Christians. By this time they were just a nuisance to the Egyptian Government. If an Italian, for example, committed a crime in Alexandria, he could insist that his trial should take place before a court in his own country. A new law in Egypt could not be carried out until it was first approved by the governments of all the countries represented there. Very often this was impossible. It took years to get them all to agree that foreign residents in Egypt should pay taxes.

There was also the Caisse de la Dette, which controlled Egypt's purse-strings. About half the country's revenue still went to pay foreign bond-holders. All the Great Powers were represented on the Caisse—Austria-Hungary, France, Germany, Italy and Russia, as well as Great Britain. Foreign governments could prevent Cromer from spending Egyptian money on anything they disapproved of. France and Russia, you may remember, managed to stop the British from using Egyptian money to pay for the re-conquest of the Sudan. Their representatives on the Caisse took the matter to the Mixed Courts. These were another brake on British power in Egypt. They were courts that consisted of European and Egyptian judges who dealt with cases to do with both Egyptians and Europeans. So you see that with the Capitulations, the Caisse de la Dette and the Mixed Courts, the British were certainly not free to do what they liked in Egypt.

France was the country that interfered most in the way the   89

British ran Egypt. This is easy to understand. The French had been interested in Egypt for centuries. Their influence in the country was very strong, partly because many rich Egyptians sent their sons to be educated in France. After the threat of war with Britain over Fashoda in 1898, however, the two countries became more friendly to each other. Finally in 1904 they made agreements settling past differences in many parts of the world, which led to what was called an 'Entente Cordiale', or 'friendly understanding'. One of these agreements had to do with Egypt. In return for the British giving them a free hand to take over Morocco, the French finally agreed that the British had special rights in Egypt. From then on the French stopped their constant criticism of what the British were doing in Egypt. Another result was that the Caisse de la Dette from then on became only a debt-collector for the foreign bondholders, which meant that the Egyptian Government could now manage its own finances.

DRAWBACKS OF BRITISH RULE

Reorganising the government, straightening out its finances, developing trade, *irrigation*, and communications, improving health, working conditions, law and order, as well as over-hauling the army—from all of these changes the Egyptians benefited under Lord Cromer. Yet few Egyptians were at all grateful or wanted the British to stay. Some said that the British did not do enough to develop industry, such as cloth-making, which would have provided work for the many unemployed; instead, they said, the British selfishly encouraged the Egyptians only to grow cotton in order to supply cotton-spinners in Britain. By concentrating on this one crop many people in Egypt were thrown out of work when after 1907 there was a slump in the demand for raw cotton. Others said that the British did very little to help the very poor people of Egypt, but allowed the rich pashas to get even richer.

Another criticism of British rule was that the British did not give the Egyptians enough training in how to run their own country. It is true that there was an Egyptian Government,

90

with a prime minister and other ministers, but like the Khedive they were guided at every turn by British advisers. Once the Khedive tried to change his ministers, but he was stopped by Cromer and told not to do it again. Originally it had been intended that Egypt should be ruled with 'British heads and Egyptian hands'. This meant that Egyptians should carry out the running of their own affairs with British senior civil servants to help for a while. In fact the number of Britons working in Egypt for the Government increased. In 1885 there were only about a hundred; twenty years later there were over a thousand. One observer said that after years of British rule the Egyptians were probably less ready for self-government than they had been before.

The British always said that there were just not enough educated and experienced Egyptians to govern the country. This was partly their own fault. They did not encourage the Egyptian Government to spend enough money on schools. It was often left to private individuals or organisations such as churches or missionary societies to set up schools and supply teachers. Most Egyptians could not read or write. Very few girls went to school. Boys were sometimes sent to primary schools, run by the local mosque, but there they learned only to recite the *Koran*. The few secondary schools were for preparing boys to become clerks. There was very little higher education, especially in technical subjects. It was not until 1909 that a new university was founded to teach modern subjects and train men for professions. The ancient university of Al-Azhar in Cairo was only for religious studies. Altogether the British badly neglected education during their occupation.

In criticising the British for what they failed to do, it is wise to remember that for many years they genuinely intended to leave Egypt as soon as possible. After making sure that the Suez Canal was safe, their first aim was to make Egypt strong enough to pay its own way. This took longer than expected. Then, as we have seen, they found they had to conquer the Sudan. Finally they came to think of Egypt as vital for the security of their Empire in India. If they left, they imagined, another country, such as France, would surely try to take it over. And so, the longer they stayed, the more difficult it was for the British to leave.

You might ask why the British did not make Egypt a colony. Then they would have been able to do what they liked and introduce all the improvements they wanted. No British Government ever seems to have seriously considered this. For one thing it would have been very costly and many people at home would have been against the idea. Besides, the other Great Powers would have objected, and Britain would soon have had all sorts of trouble with other nations if she had tried to take over Egypt completely. In fact there were many British people who wanted the Government to leave Egypt altogether. One of the most outspoken was the poet Wilfrid Scawen Blunt. He was a great lover of the Arabs and lived for many years in Egypt. In letters, speeches, lectures and pamphlets he kept on saying that British rule in Egypt was bad and urging the Government to end the occupation.

THE NATIONALISTS

By the turn of the century more and more Egyptians themselves were telling the British to go. Chief among them were the members of the Nationalist Party. They were highly educated young men, many of them lawyers who had been trained in France, who felt discontented that there were not enough opportunities for them in politics under British rule. Their cry was 'Egypt for the Egyptians'. They wanted a government of their own and a parliament elected by the people of Egypt. Lord Cromer had little time for the Nationalists. He once said that to appoint one of them to rule Egypt was 'as little less absurd as the nomination of some savage Red Indian Chief to be Governor-General of Canada'. Yet not long before his retirement from Egypt he made one of them Minister of Education, so strong had the Nationalists become. This was Saad Zaghlul Pasha. About twenty years later he became the most outstanding Prime Minister Egypt had ever had. In the meantime, however, the Nationalists could only show their discontent by making speeches, organising demonstrations and writing articles for the newspapers. In the early years of this century they made the most of the ill-feeling that was steadily rising against the British throughout Egypt.

DENSHAWAI

This ill-feeling came quickly to the surface in 1906. One day in June a group of about six British officers took time off *manoeuvres* in the Delta to go pigeon-shooting near the little village of Denshawai, at the invitation of the local sheikh. They were in uniform at the time, and while they waited for the sheikh to turn up they found themselves surrounded by angry villagers who objected to their pigeons being shot. The soldiers could speak no Arabic and the local people did not understand any English. In the confusion that followed a rifle went off and several villagers were wounded. The soldiers were then set upon with sticks. One of them managed to escape back to camp, where he raised the alarm. On their way back to the village they found one of the officers, Captain Bull, dead on the ground, the result of head-wounds and sunstroke. At this they seized one of the villagers and beat him to death.

Denshawai: flogging the culprits

An enquiry was held and fifty-two peasants were brought to trial for the murder of the British officer. The court consisted of British and Egyptian judges, presided over by an Egyptian who was under British direction. They found most of the villagers not guilty, but the rest were punished severely. Most were either sent to do hard labour in prison or given fifty lashes. Four were actually hanged in public. There was an immediate outcry both in Egypt and abroad against such punishments. Though Lord Cromer was not in Egypt at the time, his enemies blamed him for not stopping the sentences from being carried out. He later admitted that they had been 'though not unjust, unduly severe'.

The Denshawai incident spoiled Cromer's last year in Egypt. Many people forgot all the good that he had done for the country. He was a very aloof man in public but he did have a genuine desire to help the mass of the Egyptian people to get out of their wretched poverty. Few gave him much credit for this. Probably one of his greatest mistakes was that he did not try to win over the leaders of Egyptian nationalism by giving them jobs in the government. He always thought that he knew what was best for the people. And so when he left Cairo for the last time he drove away through deserted streets.

WINTER IN EGYPT

One of the pleasanter sides of Cromer's Egypt was the growth of tourism. Every year between November and April steamers would land hundreds of tourists at Alexandria and Port Said. Around 1900 it became very fashionable to 'winter' in Egypt.

Tourists came not only to enjoy Egypt's warm, sunny winters, they came also to see the remarkable remains of Egypt's ancient past. *Archaeologists* had carefully *excavated* and restored many of the tombs and temples dating back thousands of years to the time of the Pharaohs. No tour of Egypt was complete without a trip to the Pyramids. Many people came to Egypt to see a place they had all read about in their Bibles. They wanted to see for themselves the country of Joseph and his Brethren, and of Moses and the Children of Israel. Others were just curious to see a land that was only then being opened up to visitors.

A tour of Egypt cost a great deal of money, especially for people who liked to travel on their own. It was cheaper to go on a tour arranged by a travel agent. Thomas Cook & Son, who had been running tours to Egypt since 1889, offered one that cost £120, all inclusive. It lasted twelve weeks and took in Palestine as well. Baedeker's Guide-book to Egypt said that in three weeks it was possible to get only a 'glimpse' of Egypt, there was so much to see there. Obviously only very wealthy people could afford to go there.

One of the most popular ways of travelling to Egypt was by *P. & O.* liner. One left London every week on its voyage to India, calling in at Port Said on the way through the Suez Canal. The journey to Egypt took just under a fortnight and cost £20 single, £32 return, first class. Some people preferred to travel across Europe by train and catch a boat at Marseilles or one of the other Mediterranean ports.

Once through the Customs, tourists generally made straight for Cairo, putting up at one of the city's many fine hotels. The most fashionable and oldest established was the famous Shepheard's Hotel. Generations of British servicemen, as well as tourists, knew Shepheard's of Cairo. Its staff claimed that it could cater for every kind of guest.

Most visitors wanted to go sight-seeing. They could go about Cairo quite safely on their own, either on foot, or, better for the dusty, crowded streets of the Old Town, on a donkey. There were so many donkeys that they had to have number plates! Baedeker's Guide-book warned travellers that if they employed a guide, or *dragoman* as he was called, they 'would avoid all the petty annoyances incident to direct dealings with the natives', but they would have to watch out he did not cheat them of their money.

Tourists often made straight for the Citadel, that ancient fortress built by Saladin, ruler of Egypt in the time of Richard the Lion-heart during the Crusades. Nearby were many mosques with beautiful tile and *mosaic* decoration to admire.

Dark streets of Cairo. Notice the open shops on the left

Over to the west beside the Nile was the New Town. Here were many palaces to see and pleasure-gardens in which to stroll. Tourists had many ways to pass the time. They could go duck-shooting, play golf, tennis or polo, or go to the races. Many were content to spend the afternoons sitting with a light refreshment on the terrace of Shepheard's, watching the fascinating crowds pass by. Evenings might be spent at the Opera or at any of Cairo's many famous restaurants. Some of these, however, were hardly suitable for ladies. They were the favourite haunts of British soldiers from the barracks in the town.

For some travellers the highlight of their visit to Egypt was an excursion in a steamer up the Nile. This could be most relaxing, though there were many sight-seeing tours by donkey-ride on the way. Among the most outstanding sights were the giant figures carved out of the rock on the river's side at Abu Simbel. Another was the beautiful ruined temple of Isis on the island of Philae. The ruins were partly submerged by the waters of the Nile as a result of the building of the dam at Aswan.

Cairo, the Citadel with the mosque of Mohamed Ali. Notice the size of the houses in the foreground

British tourists on the verandah of Shepheard's Hotel, Cairo

Engineers dismantling the giant statues at Abu Simbel

Back in Cairo again before leaving for home, tourists might go back to the Old Town to venture into the many crowded, dark *bazaars*. There they could buy leather goods, copper ware and brass work, some of it still made by local craftsmen, much of it already mass-produced and imported from abroad. Tourists had to be ready to *haggle* for what they wanted; stall-keepers always charged high prices. It might take days to strike a bargain and then settle a price over a tiny cup of thick, strong Turkish coffee.

European visitors hardly ever went into the countryside and so they rarely got to know the fellahin. In the towns they came into contact mainly with the other people of Egypt, the Jews, *Copts*, Turks or some of the many Europeans who had long settled here. Guide-books like Baedeker did not encourage visitors to try to get to know the local people. They were told, 'Intimate acquaintance with Orientals is to be avoided, *disinterested* friendship being still rarer in the East than elsewhere. The average Oriental regards the European traveller as a *Croesus*, and, sometimes too as a madman – so unintelligible to him are the objects of travelling.' Visitors ought always to be firm and cautious, but they 'should bear in mind that many of the natives are mere children, whose waywardness should excite *compassion* rather than anger, and who often display a touching simplicity and kindliness of *disposition*.' We do not read what the Egyptians thought of their visitors.

9 Egypt since Lord Cromer

The British had much to do with Egypt long after 1907 when Lord Cromer left. Unfortunately, relations between the two countries got worse instead of better. His successors, it is true, tried to help the people of Egypt; one of them even set up a kind of parliament, so that they could have some say in the government of their country, but it never represented the ordinary people of Egypt, and its members were rich landowners who seemed interested only in making themselves even richer at the country's expense. The good intentions of British officials were not appreciated, and most Egyptians remained horribly poor and ignorant. Politicians spent most of their time urging the British to go.

For a time the British tightened their grip on Egypt. During the First World War the British and Turks were fighting on opposite sides, and so in 1914 the British took over Egypt as a Protectorate. For the next eight years they treated Egypt as a colony. Their troops used it freely as a base for defending the Suez Canal and for fighting the Turks. Egyptian Nationalists who spoke out against the British were *deported*.

When the war was over Egyptians, led by the Nationalist leader Saad Zaghlul, went to Paris where the great Peace Conference was being held. They demanded for Egyptians the right to rule their own country as they wanted. As the Turkish Empire had broken up as a result of the recent war the British declared Egypt an independent kingdom in 1922.

But Egypt was not really independent. It was only one of several 'puppet' states, or disguised colonies, that the British had set up in what had just been the Turkish Empire – Palestine, (the modern Israel), Transjordan, (now called Jordan) and Iraq. The British still kept an army in Egypt with a fleet stationed at Alexandria. Through their representative in Cairo they were more or less able to rule Egypt as before.

This was shown very clearly during the Second World War. Though the Egyptians insisted on staying neutral they were forced to co-operate with the British, who once again used Egypt as a base for fighting their enemies, this time the Germans and Italians. One of the fiercest and most important battles of this war was fought in Egypt in 1942. This was the Battle of el Alamein.

After 1945 the Egyptians determined to be free of British control once for all. From 1948 they were off and on at war with the new state of Israel. The fighting went very badly for Egypt. Many Egyptians blamed King Farouk, who was lazy, corrupt and inefficient. In 1952 a group of army officers seized power and forced him to *abdicate*. As a result of this revolution a republic was set up. One of the officers who planned it rose to power as president. This was Colonel Gamal Abdel Nasser.

Under their new leaders the Egyptians pressed the British to withdraw their troops. The British still had bases in Egypt even after giving up India in 1947. They were there to guard the Suez Canal which was thought vital for the passage of British warships in time of any war, and supplies of precious oil at all times from the Persian Gulf oil wells. After many lengthy talks the British agreed first to withdraw their troops to the Canal Zone, then from Egypt altogether in 1954. After seventy-two years of occupation the British finally left.

Two years later they were back. President Nasser was very ambitious to modernise Egypt and also to unite all Arabs and free them from foreign domination. The British Government of Sir Anthony Eden did not trust Nasser. In the summer of 1956 Nasser suddenly announced he was taking over the Suez Canal from its French owners. He said that he would use the money paid in shipping dues to build a new high dam at Aswan. This would generate enough electricity to power Egypt's new industries, that would bring work and prosperity to millions. In

Britain many people feared that the Egyptians would not have enough pilots to run the Canal efficiently, others were afraid that Nasser might not let British ships use it. A great many were also indignant that he had taken it over without consulting either the owners or the British Government. The governments of Britain and France determined to get the Canal out of Nasser's hands. They said that they were interested only in seeing that it was put under international control for the benefit of all countries. In secret, however, they made plans to attack Egypt.

They decided to co-operate with the Israelis. In the autumn of 1956 the Israelis invaded Egypt to stop Arab *guerrillas* attacking Israel. By secret arrangement the British and French intervened, only to protect the Suez Canal, they said, by separating the two fighting armies. When the Egyptians refused to stop fighting, British and French troops landed at Port Said to take over the Canal.

They went no further, however. In the United Nations Organisation the two countries were condemned for attacking Egypt by most of the other countries. Even their allies, the Americans, turned against them. Before long, therefore, British and French forces had to be withdrawn from Port Said.

In Britain there was a great deal of argument about what the Government had done. Some people supported the Prime Minister. They said that President Nasser was an enemy of Britain and were quite prepared to defy the rest of the world. When British troops were withdrawn they thought that this was a defeat for Britain. Others said that it was not right for the Egyptians to *nationalise* the Canal without consulting the owners, the Suez Canal Company, but that it was wrong for Britain to attack Egypt. They said that it was sheer madness to land troops at Port Said because it had only led to Egyptians blocking the Canal. If Britain did not take her troops away quickly she would become involved in a full-scale war against the rest of the world with only the French and the Israelis for allies.

Obviously the Suez Crisis of 1956 only made relations between Britain and Egypt worse than ever. To many British people, especially ex-servicemen who thought they knew Egypt well, the Egyptians were still only 'Gippos' or 'Wogs', to be looked down on as lazy, dirty and unreliable. Egyptians who wanted to make their country modern, independent and respected in the world, thought that the British were living in the past in the days of the British Empire. Britain just could not bully a weak country like Egypt any more.

Though they were sometimes successful in ruling people in other parts of the world it is curious how the British failed to get on well with the people of Egypt. In India and parts of Africa they were able to show the best side, the benefits of British rule. In Egypt they showed mostly their worst side, their lack of feeling for what the people wanted most, freedom to rule themselves. Perhaps they were not given the chance to show their better side. At any rate, it will probably be many years before the two peoples forget the time spent by the British as rulers in Egypt.

How Do We Know?

Any time you read a history book you ought to say to yourself, 'How does the author know it was like this?' He could not be there to find out for himself, so how can he tell? A historian has to rely upon what other people at the time wrote about what they did and saw. What they wrote, in diaries, reports, letters or memoirs are what are called his sources of information. Sometimes a historian finds that other historians have used these sources already and he may be very grateful to them, because he can use their books as a guide in his own research. But wherever possible, a historian tries to read the original sources as well and make up his own mind what things were like in the past.

Many of the people who visited Egypt in the nineteenth century wrote about what they saw and did. You will probably have read about some of them already. Lady Lucie Duff Gordon was one. Her 'Letters from Egypt' were published by her daughter. Stanley Lane-Poole also spent a long time in Egypt and wrote about his experiences in 'Social Life in Egypt'. Both these writers tell us about the everyday life of ordinary Egyptians. So does R. Talbot Kelly in a little book for young people called 'Peeps at Many Lands: Egypt'. He was an artist and he illustrated his book with some of his paintings, which also are a useful source of information, as you can see in this book. (Many of the other pictures in this book were drawn by artists living at the time but not on the spot. They took great care, however, to make their pictures as accurate as possible.)

As more and more people went to Egypt for holidays tourist guides were written. Two of the earliest and best were Karl Baedeker's famous guides to Upper and Lower Egypt. These are fascinating books to read. If you use your imagination you can almost feel you have been to Egypt a hundred years ago, so full are they of detailed information about all that a tourist might want to know.

As you know, not only tourists from Britain went to Egypt. People who were interested in de Lesseps' Suez Canal were eager to read such a work as Percy Fitzgerald's 'The Great Canal at Suez' or 'Recollections of Forty Years', that de Lesseps wrote himself. Politicians, as you know, were particularly concerned about Egypt. This can be seen in documents specially prepared for them known as 'Parliamentary Papers', which are full of reports and messages from Egypt. We can read what leading politicians said about Egypt at the time in their letters, which can most easily be found in biographies of such men as Disraeli and Gladstone. The letters and reports of soldiers like Gordon, Wolseley, Kitchener and Winston Churchill also tell us a lot about Egypt. Accounts written by Englishmen who governed Egypt are also useful; Sir Edward Milner in 'England in Egypt' and Lord Cromer in 'Modern Egypt' are two examples. Both are very serious works; much more amusing to read are Lord Edward Cecil's 'The Leisure of an Egyptian Official' and 'Orientations' by Sir Edward Storrs.

Most of these books would be very hard for you to read, even if you could lay your hands on them. Some of them are kept in libraries that are not open to the general public, others are out of print, though you could be as lucky as I was and find one or two in second-hand book-shops. To help you find out more about the British in Egypt for yourself here is a list of books that you are more likely to find in bookshops and libraries:

Burchell, S. C., 'Building the Suez Canal'. Cassell (Caravel Books); Hogg, Garry, 'Suez Canal: a link between two seas'. Hutchinson; Hobley, L. F., 'Opening Africa'. Methuen (Outlines); Ellis, H. B., 'The Arab'. Brockhampton; Kay, Shirley, 'The Arab World'. Oxford Children's Reference Library; Henty, G.H. With Kitchener in the Soudan'. Blackie; Clark, R. W., 'Sir Winston Churchill'. (Living Biographies Series) Phoenix House; Smith, N. D., 'Winston Churchill'. Methuen (Outlines); 'Gordon at Khartoum'. (Jackdaws) Cape; 'Children's Britannica' for articles on General Gordon, Egypt and the Sudan; 'Oxford Junior Encyclopedia' for articles on Gordon, Kitchener and the Egyptians.

Things to Do

1 Draw up a *prospectus* or write a speech that Ferdinand de Lesseps might have written about 1858 to encourage people to support his plans for the Suez Canal. If you had been a financier or shipowner would you have been interested?

2 Write some imaginary letters to the newspaper that might have appeared at the time to show how people disagreed about (*a*) Disraeli's purchase of the Suez Canal shares in 1875; (*b*) the British invasion and occupation of Egypt in 1882; (*c*) Kitchener's campaign in the Sudan in 1898.

3 Read more about General Gordon in some of the many biographies written on him. Hold a mock trial of Gladstone for the death of Gordon at Khartoum.

4 You would possibly enjoy reading A. E. W. Mason's 'The Four Feathers', an adventure story about the Sudan in the time of Gordon and Kitchener. Look out for the film of the same name that was made many years ago.

5 The poem by Rudyard Kipling quoted on page 80 is taken from a collection of his poems, entitled 'Barrack Room Ballads'. Read some of them to get an idea of how people felt about belonging to the British Empire around 1900.

6 Find out as much as you can about the part your local regiment may have played in campaigns in Egypt.

7 Write an *obituary* of Lord Cromer that might have appeared in 1917 (*a*) in an Egyptian Nationalist newspaper; (b) in a British newspaper.

8 Find out more about the Suez Crisis of 1956. Look up newspapers of the time that may be kept in a public library; ask people who remember the events well. Make up your own mind about the rights and wrongs of the British Government's action.

9 Make a scrap-book of pictures, post-cards and news items about Egypt and the Suez Canal. Ask people who have lived in Egypt or sailed through the Canal what it was like.

10 Imagine you are a tourist in Egypt about 1900. Write a diary or letters home about what you are seeing. Look up books about ancient Egypt to find out about the temples, pyramids, etc. you would be visiting.

11 Try to find books about the exploration of the Nile *or* about the Sudan desert. Write an adventure story *either* about exploring the Nile *or* about getting lost in the desert.

Glossary

to abdicate, to give up being a king
Admiralty, government department to do with the Royal Navy
affluence, wealth
archaeologist, one who studies the past from ancient remains
Balkans, south-eastern Europe north of Greece
bankrupt, unable to pay one's debts
barrage, dam
barrister, lawyer who argues a case in an English law court
battery, group of guns
bazaar, Eastern market-place
Bedouin, wandering Arab of the desert
benefactor, one who helps others
benighted, ignorant
the Black Watch, a Scottish Highland regiment
Boers, settlers of Dutch origin living in South Africa
bondholder, person holding bonds, written promises to pay
brigade, body of troops consisting of at least two regiments
Cabinet, chief members of the government
cataract, waterfall
cholera, deadly infectious disease
Civil List, money set aside for the ruler's personal expenses
cob, head of corn
compassion, pity
concession, grant
consul-general, chief agent of a foreign country who helps businessmen
consumption, disease of the lungs
convention, temporary agreement
Copts, Christian Egyptians
courbash, long leather whip
creditors, people to whom money is owed
Croesus, fabulously rich man
decimated, cut down very heavily

deported, sent into exile

Diamond Jubilee, sixtieth anniversary of coming to the throne

dictator, ruler who can do as he likes in his own country

diplomat, one who represents his country abroad

to disembark, to land from a ship

disinterested, unselfish

dispatch, message

disposition, character

dividend, money paid out to a shareholder

division, an army unit made up of two brigades

dragoman, guide

eltchi, Turkish for ambassador

evacuation, withdrawal from

excavated, dug out

exorbitant, much too great a price (or demand)

exploited, made to work solely for another's benefit

fellahin, Arabic for lowly peasants

financier, man dealing in very large sums of money

flotilla, a fleet of small boats

Foreign Secretary, member of Government dealing with foreign
  countries

garrison, soldiers guarding a fortress

grapeshot, shot from gun that scatters when fired

guerrillas, soldiers who attack the enemy in small groups

gum, kind of resin from a tree

to haggle, to be slow to make a bargain

hindermost, farthest behind

hodmen, labourers

howitzer, short squat gun used for shelling

humus, valuable part of soil

hypocrite, person who hides his true character, who says one thing and
  means another

to incur, to bring on oneself, to undertake

infidel, person who believes in another religion

intelligence officer, soldier who collects information

interest, money paid for a sum borrowed until it is repaid

irrigated, made fertile by artificial supplies of water

irrigation, method of making ground fertile

isthmus, narrow neck of land joining two larger pieces of land

khalifa, Arabic title, meaning successor

khedive, title of rulers of Egypt from 1867 to 1922, meaning prince

Koran, Muslim holy book

lateen, large triangular sail

to liberate, to free

lurid, sensational, exaggerated

mania, mad fondness

manifesto, statement of aims and intentions

manoeuvres, army exercises

maritime, to do with the sea

Middle East, group of countries lying between the Mediterranean Sea
and the Indian Ocean

mirage, trick of the atmosphere by which things in distance seem to be
hanging in the air

to monopolise, to take over and be the only holder

monstrosity, horribly wrong

mortar, cement of lime, sand and water

mortgaged, handed over as security for debt

mosaic, pattern made of small pieces of cemented marble or glass

mosque, place where Muslims worship

to nationalise, to take over for the people of a country

Nile Delta, land at the mouth of River Nile

obituary, account written about a person who has just died

ours, French for bear

P. & O., short for Peninsular and Oriental, a shipping company

Pasha, Turkish governor

pavilion, large ornamental tent

Paymaster-General, junior member of the Government

to perceive, to see

perennial, lasting throughout the year

to perpetrate, to commit, or do (usually something bad)

pestilence, deadly disease

pharaoh, ruler of Egypt in ancient times

pillaged, plundered, stolen from

pipkin, small earthenware cooking-pot

pith, marrow from stem of certain plants

plantation, estate in tropical country for cultivating crops

the Powers, most powerful countries in the world

prospectus, outline of a plan

reconnaissance, preliminary survey

to reconnoitre, to spy out the land, make a reconnaissance

redoubtable, very strong, valiantly defended

reinforcements, soldiers sent to help

to renounce, to give up claim

report, noise of gunfire
resolved, decided
retrograded, fallen from better to worse
revenue, money brought in
sakia, water-wheel
sand-spit, long narrow sand-bank
to scrutinise, to look at very closely
seconded, transferred for a short time
serge, tough woollen cloth
shaduf, water-crane
sheikh, Arab chief
sickle, sharp curved tool for cutting grass or corn
solvency, being able to pay
sovereign, old British gold coin worth £1
spurious, false
starveling, thin
Sultan, ruler of the Turkish Empire
to suppress, to put down
to till, to cultivate land
toll, payment for the right to pass
transaction, business deal
Treasury, government department in charge of country's money
tumult, loud roar
unbelievers, non-Muslims
usurious, far too high
veneered, disguised
to whittle away, to reduce
wrought, worked
zeriba, stockade made of thorn bushes

Acknowledgements

The author would like to thank Messrs. J. Scott Allan and Eric J. Simpson for reading the book in manuscript and for making many helpful criticisms. He is grateful also to Mrs. Mary Kennoway of Moray House College of Education Library for compiling the reading list in 'How Do We Know?' The author and publisher are also grateful to the following for permission to reproduce copyright material: Asia Publishing House Ltd for an extract from *Founders of Modern Egypt* by Mary Rowlett; The Hamlyn Publishing Group Ltd. for an extract from *River War* by Winston Churchill and Authors agent, Mrs. George Bambridge and Methuen & Co. Ltd, for an extract from "Fuzzy Wuzzy" in *Barrack Room Ballads* by Rudyard Kipling.

For permission to reproduce illustrative material we are grateful to the following ·

Page

6 *Lady Duff Gordon's letters from Egypt* R. Brimley & Johnson, 1902
7 Kelly *Egypt* A & C Black, 1903
8 *top* S. Lane-Poole *Social Life in Egypt*, 1884 *bottom* Radio Times Hulton Picture Library (R.T.H.P.L.)
10 S. Lane Poole *op. cit.*
13 R.T.H.P.L.
15 R.T.H.P.L.
17 R.T.H.P.L.
18 R.T.H.P.L.
19 R.T.H.P.L.
20 R.T.H.P.L.
21 R.T.H.P.L.
22 Illustrated London News (I.L.N.)
23 R.T.H.P.L.
26 R.T.H.P.L.
28 R.T.H.P.L.
29 Punch
33 Mansell Collection
35 R.T.H.P.L.
38 Mansell Collection
40 Mansell Collection
41 Mansell Collection
43 R.T.H.P.L.

47 R.T.H.P.L.
48 R.T.H.P.L.
51 R.T.H.P.L.
53 Mansell Collection
58 I.L.N.
59 I.L.N.
61 British Museum
63 I.L.N.
65 Leeds City Art Galleries
68 R.T.H.P.L.
73 Bassano and Vandyk Studios
75 R.T.H.P.L.
76 W. S. Churchill *The River War* Longman, 1900
79 R.T.H.P.L.
81 H. Roger Viollet
85 R.T.H.P.L.
87 R.T.H.P.L.
93 I.L.N.
96 D. Roberts *Egypt and Nubia*, 1849
97 Paul Popper Ltd.
98 *top* Paul Popper Ltd *bottom* Unesco
102 Keystone Press Agency